D1737188

ALLUMETTE ISLAND
MASSACRE

KEITH LANDRY

Copyright © 2019 by Keith Landry

All rights reserved.

No part of this book may be reproduced in any form or by any electronic or
mechanical means, including information storage and retrieval systems,
without written permission from the author, except for the use of brief
quotations in a book review.

Special thanks to my wife Vivian, my friend Stephen Duggan, Michael Landry, and Gina Jestadt for their generous assistance in the publication of this book.

Thanks to Marc Landry for the front cover photo.

Keith Landry www.keithhlandy.com

Gina Jestadt specializes in helping writers become authors through self-publishing . Visit her website www.joosepublishing.info

PREFACE

This book contains the true story of a massacre that occurred in the 1930s in western Quebec. It tells the story of Michael Bradley, a man who shot to death five members of his own family. The investigation, trials, and hanging were the most-followed crime news of the 1930s.

Readers will be mesmerized by the investigators' efforts to solve the case and to satisfy a jury to render a conviction as well as the real courtroom drama that followed to serve justice.

This story was first published in the book Allumette Island Massacre and Three Other Canadian Crime Stories. This is a rewrite with only the Allumette Island Massacre story.

CONTENTS

PART I
MURDER INVESTIGATION

1. Campbell's Bay, Quebec 3
2. My Grandparents 7
3. The Story Begins 13
4. Driving to Allumette Island 15
5. Preliminary Investigation 25
6. The Coroner Arrives 35
7. The Detectives Arrive 37
8. Michael Bradley 41
9. Home 51
10. Meeting in the Morning 53
11. Fetching Michael Bradley 55
12. Autopsy 57
13. The Inquest 63
14. Dalpe Speaks to the Press 67
15. The Statement 69
16. Father's Sermon 73
17. Breakfast 77
18. Rifle 81
19. More Evidence 87
20. Bradley Confesses 91
21. Supper at the St. Germain Home 95
22. Inquest Part 2 99
23. Preliminary Hearing 103

PART II
CAMPBELL'S BAY MURDER TRIAL

24. Trial Excitement Begins 109
25. Transporting Michael Bradley 113
26. Trial's First Day 115

27. Second Day   119
28. Third Day   123
29. Fourth Day   125
30. Fifth Day   129
31. Sixth Day - Trial Closings   131
32. The Verdict   139
33. Beverage Room Talk   143

PART III
RETRIAL

34. Monday, January 6, 1935   147
35. Confession Admissible   151
36. Bradley Statements and Confession   153
37. Thursday, January 9, 1935   155
38. Closing Arguments   157
39. A Very Different Justice's Charge   161
40. The Verdict   167
41. Sentencing   169
42. Speaking to Journalists   173
43. Meeting the Attorney General   175
44. Final Chapter – The Hanging   177

Some after Notes   181
About the Author   183

ONTARIO

Pontiac County

I

MURDER INVESTIGATION

1

CAMPBELL'S BAY, QUEBEC

My parents dropped me, Keith, age 11, and my younger brother, John, age 7, to stay for a couple of weeks with our grandparents in the Village of Campbell's Bay, Quebec. It was early July 1961.

Our parents were leaving to drive to Port Colborne in southern Ontario. Port Colborne is where the Welland Canal connects Lake Erie to Lake Ontario. They were going to visit my father's two brothers and a sister who lived there. They had placed my two older brothers in Camp Ave Maria, which was on the Ottawa River near Arnprior, Ontario. It was to be their holiday away from their four boys.

Campbell's Bay was founded in 1904 and named for Lieutenant Campbell of the Scottish Regiment that settled there in 1851. It was a logging and sawmill town until the mill closed in the 1940s.

The village is about 3.5 sq. kms. and is built on a slight hill that runs from its north end down to the Ottawa River at its south. There are three entrances to the town, one each on the east, west, and north sides, all sloping down to the Main Street, which is on level ground. There are four blocks of housing that run south from Main Street to the Ottawa River. These houses rest on level land.

The town had a small retail presence with shops like the Five and Dime Department store, a grocer, two hotels with beverage rooms, and a restaurant. The Legion was located on Main Street and provided a gathering spot for World War I and II veterans.

The population of the village in 1961 was around 1,000 people, mainly of French and Irish ancestry, making it primarily a Catholic village. At the west end of Main Street there is the small white Catholic church with its steeple. A little farther into the countryside is the Catholic cemetery. There were a few English Canadian families and a Protestant church and cemetery on the east end of town.

Campbell's Bay Today Photo by P.199 at Wikimedia Commons

The most notorious event in Campbell's Bay's history took place on April 5, 1935, when Michael Bradley was hung by the neck until dead after being convicted of the murder of five of his family members. It was the first and last hanging in Campbell's Bay. This story is based on true events.

2

MY GRANDPARENTS

My grandmother, Edna, was 59 years of age in 1961. She always seemed very old to me. She had been a beauty in her day, but she was short, maybe 5 feet tall, and had put on weight. Her hair was now as white as snow. She had preserved her beautiful oval face featuring the largest deep blue eyes you could imagine.

She was kindly to us when we visited. But she was not the hugging type. While we were there, she was always checking to see if we had our daily bowel movements. That seemed to be her greatest concern about us. Even when we confirmed we had, she seemed skeptical that we were telling the truth.

What we missed most about being away from home was our access to foods we were accustomed to. At home we would have sugared cereals, toast with butter, and our favorite jams. Grandma served bran cereal, half a grapefruit with a sprinkle of sugar, and toast with marmalade. Worst was the oleo used as a replacement for butter. My brother and I had to squeeze the yellow coloring into the margarine to have it look more like butter.

Picture of my Grandparents, 1923

We never starved, so I am assuming it was not always so unappealing. Lunch was baloney sandwiches instead of peanut butter and jam sandwiches. Supper might be fried spam and, on Friday, always fish out of respect to our Catholic faith. Whatever my grandma made, John and I would frown upon it. She was not one to coddle; so, if you left your food, you went hungry.

Thank God for my grandmother's sweet tooth, because dessert at supper was usually ice cream and or cake. Yes!

My grandfather, a handsome man named Michael, was 75 years old in 1961. He had a square chin on a large square head, piercing eyes, and a high tight buzz cut. He was always clean-shaven. He was tall and muscular, a large man with broad shoulders.

He also seemed old to me because he had white hair, smoked a pipe (and cigarettes when my grandmother was out), and most importantly, he always seemed to be sleeping in his chair in the living room. He was forgetful, often struggling to remember our names. Years later, I would learn that he had the beginnings of dementia. My grandfather had been a prominent person throughout the Pontiac County. Many years earlier, he had been the county's high constable reporting to the county sheriff and responsible for the county constables. Constables served writs and warrants, guarded the county jail, and made arrests.

Michael was also one of the toughest men in the area. I have heard stories through the years from family members and others from the county that my grandfather was called upon by area beverage room owners to come and break up fights. The two stories I recall best were when he banged the heads of two rowdies in the Campbell's Bay bar and another when someone from outside of the area came to a picnic to pick a fight with him and was quickly sent packing by my grandfather.

My grandfather was a businessman who owned properties and logging trucks, which he rented to area sawmills.

My grandmother was my grandfather's second wife. His first wife died in 1918, leaving him with four young children. One child died at the age of 6 when she had an allergy attack after eating some candy that she had just bought at the village's convenience store. My grandfather brought the remaining three children into his new marriage in 1921 for my grandmother to help raise. He was 38 years old, and she was 21. My mother was born in 1925, their only shared child. During the 1940s, my grandparents also adopted my grandmother's niece when her sister passed away giving birth to the little girl.

Their home was a duplex. My grandparents lived on one side, and the other side was rented out.

The house had white wooden siding that ran parallel to the ground. The front door faced north and was off the front living room. There was also an entrance to the house through the kitchen. That entrance opened to a veranda, which looked down on a road with a V-shaped curve. The rectangular house sat within the boundaries of that sharp curve. During the late evenings you could hear daredevils screeching their tires as they tried to navigate the curve at high speeds.

The front of the house was built on the side of a hill that slanted steeply from the north to the south side of the house. The living room and dining room sat on the hillside while the kitchen sat over a garage where the hill gave way to a level area. The kitchen end of the house was held up by strong wooden beams. The beams were longer at the back of the house where the kitchen was and the surface below became flat. There were no beams needed in the front but, gradually as you worked your way to the back, shorter beams became larger ones.

My Grandparents House

The veranda off the kitchen was narrow and ran 30 feet from south to north. It contained a set of stairs that took you to the top of the hill and directly to the street. There were two fairly large wooden chairs on the veranda, one being a rocker, that my grandparents would use on nice days. This was where we entered the house. My grandparents kept the front door locked at all times.

There was a dining room between the kitchen and the front living room. A staircase in the dining room provided access to the second floor. At the top of the stairs, to the right, were two bedrooms with one main entrance, the first bedroom occupied by my grandparents and the second a smaller room where John and I shared a bedroom. If you turned left at the top of the stairs, you would enter a third small bedroom, which had the only bathroom in the house off it. So, if I had to get up in the night to go to the bathroom, I needed to go through my grandparent's bedroom and across the hall to the third bedroom and then into the bathroom.

The other side of the duplex was probably similar, though I confess I do not ever remember ever being on the other side.

The garage had wooden panel sliding doors that opened to a cave-like area with stone walls and dirt flooring. My grandfather would have kept his horse and buggy in the garage back in the day, but now he kept his 1952 black Chevrolet Sedan there. There were also a lot of old tools stored on dusty shelves.

3

THE STORY BEGINS

The second day into our stay, after John and I had lunch, my grandmother said she was going out for tea with one of her friends. She told us we were to remain in the house until she returned. We were to sit in the living room with grandpa and read or play cards. She would be back in a couple of hours.

So, we went in and sat on the chesterfield across from grandpa, who was already fast asleep in his chair. I had a Hardy Boys book to read, and John had some comics. After about 15 minutes, grandpa woke and stared at us while he gathered his wits.

"Who are you kids?" he mumbled.

"Grandpa, I'm Keith and this is John, Clarice's boys," I assured him.

He continued to stare, then clarity returned. He rose from his chair, and towered over us, this 230 pound, 6'2" giant of a man. He then began his story. It was a story not meant for kids our age. But it was a story that has remained with me to this day. Over the next hour, grandpa told us about his involvement in the investigation of a mass murder, the court cases, and the subsequent hanging that took place not far from their home.

Recently, I started researching these events from old newspaper clippings. The story I am about to tell you riginated with my grandfather's story that day.

4

DRIVING TO ALLUMETTE ISLAND
JULY 21, 1933

"Years ago, when I was in my prime (age 49) in the early 1930s, I was high constable of Pontiac County. I received a phone call that would impact your grandmother's and my routine for several years. It would also change our lives and that of many people in the county for many years after. Your mother was about 8 years old then.

"I received a call from Sheriff Dominic Sloan at 8:30 in the morning informing me that there had been a mass murder on Allumette Island. We needed to get there as soon as possible. Allumette Island was a drive of about an hour in those days, some 40 miles west of Campbell's Bay in western Quebec."

Allumette Island, located on the Ottawa River, is an isolated farming area. It has one village called Chapeau. The only way to get on or leave the island is by ferry to Pembroke, Ontario, or via Waltham on a bridge from the Quebec mainland at

Chapeau. Chapeau is the terminus for the Ottawa Pontiac train line.

"He (the sheriff) asked me to contact the constable in Chapeau to arrange for volunteers to set up a roadblock on the bridge leading from the Quebec highway and the ferry landing that ferried the Island people to Pembroke, Ontario."

Sheriff Sloan, who was responsible for law enforcement for the county, told grandpa he would be around to pick him up at 9 a.m. He needed to make some calls to Montreal to have Quebec Provincial Police detectives, who were experienced in this type of investigation, dispatched as soon as possible. In those days, Montreal was about a 6-hour drive from Campbell's Bay.

Grandpa continued, "I also phoned Dr. Renaud, the Campbell's Bay coroner, to meet us as soon as possible at the crime scene.

"I phoned Andre Dagenais, my Chapeau constable, and told him what the sheriff wanted. He said he'd arrange for the road block right away.

"I also contacted Tom Belanger, a constable in Campbell's Bay, to be ready to be picked up.

"The July heat had been extreme that year, and that meant high humidity for communities along the Ottawa River. That night's sleep had been like we had a blanket of humidity over us all night long."

· · ·

And the story went as follows.

Sheriff Dominique Sloan pulled his vehicle to a stop at the veranda steps to await my grandfather. He was of Irish descent, a man with bushy red hair, round clean-shaven red face, and a small but muscled physique. He was honest to the core. He was well-liked and respected and known to be smart by the area folks. He was 10 years younger than grandpa, a fit 39 years old for someone who smoked a pack of cigarettes and enjoyed a few drinks a day.

He drove a red 1932 Chevrolet for which he paid $760 brand new. He was one of the few during these depression years who could afford to buy a new car. As sheriff, his income was steady, and because he used his vehicle for law enforcement purposes, the county paid his mileage and maintenance expenses.

Grandpa opened the passenger door, said "Good morning, Dom," and received a similar greeting in return. Both men wore double-breasted light wool suits, white shirts with short collars, and ties. Both wore brogues for footwear. My grandpa's suit was brown and the sheriff's a light blue. Both men were fashionable dressers. In those days, men wore their suits from the time they rose to when they went to bed. They would also wear the same suit day after day, changing only their shirts, socks, and underwear. Periodically, the suit was sent out for dry cleaning. They placed their suit coats over the back of the front seat of the car because of the heat and kept the windows rolled down.

Mike told the sheriff to stop to pick up one of his constables, Tom Belanger.

Once there, Tom, a lanky fellow with a thin, clean-shaven face and standing about 6 feet tall, came out of his home and got in the car. He wore a grey policeman's uniform. He said good morning to the other two and asked what had happened.

Once Tom was settled in the car, Grandpa said, "Well, Dom, fill us in on what you know." Grandpa had a gravelly voice, as I recall.

Dom replied in a grave manner, "Father Harrington, curator of the Chapeau Catholic Church on Allumette Island, phoned me at around 8 a.m. to tell me that he and two other men found four bodies near Demers Center on Allumette Island. It is at Joseph Bradley's place. He said all four people had been shot dead. Apparently, a small group of men have gathered around the place.

"I told the good Father that you and I would head up there this morning. I asked him to tell the other men who have gathered around not to touch the bodies and to stay outside the parameter of the killings. I also asked that they stay around for witness statements.

"I phoned the Quebec Provincial Police right away. They are sending detectives from Hull and Montreal."

My grandfather and Constable Belanger could speak both French and English, but Sheriff Sloan could not speak French. The investigation would all be done in English.

My Grandpa replied, "Well, let's get going."

These three men were serious and thoughtful men. They discussed what they might find at the scene and what might happen when news got out to the county folks. They knew death first hand and had investigated suicides, drownings, and farm accidents but never murder. They were to enter a new phase of their law enforcement careers. Little did they realize that what happened that morning would become a major national story, resulting in journalists arriving from far outside their community. Their little part of the world would become like a circus from to time over the next two years. It would bring a boon for county retailers, hoteliers, and restaurateurs. The curious throughout the county and across the country listened for radio news or read newspapers to follow what was happening. Many turned up in the area to obtain a firsthand look at what was taking place.

The sheriff and his companions drove along Highway 148, a hilly gravel road through Fort Coulonge and on to the village of Waltham. The country air had the earthy smell of manure. They changed roads and got on the Chemin de Chapeau. The land became flatter. They drove adjacent to the Ottawa River and came to the bridge that would take them across to Allumette Island. They stopped at the bridge roadblock and spoke briefly to the fellows manning it. The men had nothing to report. The sheriff was assured that a roadblock had been set up at the ferry to Pembroke, the only other way off the Island.

They drove over the river and through the Village of Chapeau. Chapeau, Quebec, is a very small village and is the major community on Allumette Island.

Allumette Island from Allumette Island Photo Book

Chapeau Catholic Church by 199 Wikimedia Common

Chapeau has a spectacular white steeple above its Catholic Church that can be seen from the distance as you approach the village from all directions.

They proceeded south from Chapeau on Demers Center Road. On each side of the road, there were farm fields with corn and hay being grown for feed for the dairy farms located on the Island. People could be seen in the fields, starting their summer hay harvest.

Allumette Island was created when the Ottawa River receded over many years, leaving rich topsoil behind. The farms were worth more than other Pontiac County farms because the farmers could earn cash during both the summer and winter seasons. In the summer, they sold surplus hay and corn, and year around, they sold milk and butter from their dairy cows. Having said that, the 1930s had brought hardship to many of them, and selling surplus was not as prosperous as in the earlier years. The farmers' markets were in villages on both sides of the Ontario-Quebec border, the largest community being Pembroke, Ontario. It had 9,500 residences in 1933.

Farm houses were surrounded by trees and bush that provided neighbors some privacy from each other.

Some 4 miles from Chapeau, the trio arrived at Demers Center, which sits at the junction of Demers Center Road and a grid road named Wabash, which runs east west. There was a gas bar with a small confectionary and several houses.

As they drove nearer, the three men spoke of how their work might be divided. Sheriff Sloan was the senior of the three in the investigation. Of course, once the Quebec Provincial Police detectives arrived on the scene, they would become the seniors on both the investigation and the administration.

"Mike and Tom, once we arrive, I'd like to gather the potential witnesses, take their names, and see what they have to say. You and Tom can start looking around the property for clues. The detectives have a drive from Montreal of about 6 hours, so it will be awhile before they are here."

It was a hot July day, around 90 degrees Fahrenheit. During July, along the Ottawa River, the heat is stifling due to the humidity both night and day.

They reached Demers Center at 10:30 a.m. They drove past Demers Center and turned west on Wabash Road. Several 100 yards in front of them, they saw a number of men gathered at an entrance to a farmyard. Sloan pulled his Chevrolet into the yard.

A priest of medium height, dressed in his black cassock, and four men all wearing flat caps, overalls, and yellow gum boots were gathered together talking. The gum boots were ideal for the men working with livestock to protect their feet from water, mud, and manure. Their clothing was in sharp contrast to the law enforcement men's fashionable, neatly fitting suits.

Their faces wore agonizing looks. They were all smoking hand-rolled cigarettes. Everyone smoked roll-your-owns in those days.

Mr. Cantin, a farmhand who sometimes worked for Mr. Joseph Bradley, was the first to speak. All conversations that morning were in English. Excitedly, with a wild-eyed expression, this small and slight man flailed his thin arms and curled his long thin fingers when he talked.

"Three of us entered Joseph Bradley's house and found three bodies—Mrs. Mary Bradley in the kitchen, Miss Johanna Bradley in the living room, and Mr. Thomas Bradley in an upstairs bedroom."

He paused and then continued, "I found the old man Joseph's body in the stable."

Crowds Gather at Demers Center

5

PRELIMINARY INVESTIGATION

"Okay, men," the sheriff said, fixing his eyes on the potential witnesses, "You remain in the yard while Mike, Tom, and I go into the house and check out things.

"When we are done, I am going to sit at the kitchen table and take statements from each of you, one at a time, okay?"

The men nodded their heads in agreement.

The sheriff and his two associates entered the log farmhouse through the door located under an awning at the front of the home. The sheriff opened the screen door and the wooden front door and entered with Mike and Tom following. They saw a woman with a hole in her back, lying face down in a pool of blood in the middle of the living room.

"Dom, did you notice the bullet holes in the screen? Seems to me that the shooter was shooting at this woman from outside," noted Mike.

"Yes, Mike, I did," said Dom.

"Tom, you go upstairs to check on the body there and then cover it with a blanket. Bring down a couple of blankets to cover this unfortunate woman here and for the body in the kitchen," commanded Sloan. While giving the order, he pointed to a woman's body on her back on the kitchen floor. She had a bullet wound in her chest. She held a toothbrush in her right hand and a glass in the other.

"Look at this, Mike. She was brushing her teeth when she was shot," said Dom. "The shooter knew guns and how to shoot, as I see it."

Mike just gazed about, taking in what he needed to remember and then writing down some thoughts in a notebook he always carried.

Tom came down from upstairs. "It's a man, shot in the neck while he was still in bed, still with his night shirt on.

The three men then went to the log stable and found the fourth body, identified as Joseph by Father Harrington. They covered the body with a blanket. The stable had two work horses tethered in their stalls. It was a well-maintained outbuilding.

They passed the log cowshed where there were about 20 milking cows still in their stalls awaiting the morning milking.

All the bodies in the house were covered. Tom made a pot of strong coffee from the Bradleys' supplies and invited the five men in.

Sheriff Sloan sat down at one end of a large wooden kitchen table, sipping a cup of coffee.

With a grim look, the sheriff asked someone to tell him the names of each of the deceased. It was now 11:00 a.m.

Father Harrington identified them.

"Thank you, Father, now here is what is going to happen. I am going to interview each of you, one at a time. While I am interviewing one person, you others can wait outside. I will call you when it is your turn, okay?" stated the sheriff in his most serious manner.

"You can go home after I have your statement."

High Constable Michael St. Germain and Constable Tom Belanger returned to the farmyard to look for evidence.

First up was **Joseph Cantin**. He stated his name, his age as 37, and advised that he was a farm worker who lived a mile away and often worked for Joseph.

Statement from Joseph Cantin taken Friday, July 21, 1933, at 11:10 a.m.

Cantin was fidgety and nervous as he spoke.

"I started out from home at about 6:15 this morning, reaching Demers Center at 6:20 a.m. I was out looking for work. There were a few people standing around outside the confectionary. I went inside to get some tobacco, and when I came out, I heard three shots. I knew they were gunshots because I served in WWI. I stopped there about two minutes, then started toward the Bradley's house. On the way, I met Loyola Allard who told me that he had also heard five shots.

"Loyola and me, we went up to the house where the priest came up to us. Father Harrington asked me to look around. I looked in the window, and I told him the girl was dead. He then asked me to go to the back and go in and open the front door for him. That is when I seen the old lady lying in the kitchen, her daughter lying on the floor in the living room and I goes up to the bedroom upstairs and that is where I finds another body."

Second up was Father Harrington who stated his name, his age as 42 and that he was the Curator of the Chapeau Catholic Church.

Statement from Father Harrington taken Friday, July 21, 1933, beginning at 11:30 a.m.

Calmly, he began, "I was in the yard at my home getting ready to leave for Pembroke when a creamery truck driver came in and told me I was wanted at Joseph Bradley's place. The driver told me there had been a shooting there.

"I proceeded to the house where I saw Adam Allard and Joseph Cantin looking into the house. I parked my car in front of the driveway. I found the front door of the house locked. I peered through the window and saw a body, which later proved to be that of a woman. I asked Cantin to go to the back door and open the front door. When he opened it and I entered, I saw the body of a girl on the floor and an old woman in the kitchen.

"After searching the rooms, I went upstairs and saw the body of a man who I took to be Joseph Bradley. The bed was tossed and quilts scattered about. I came out and told the men to stay away until the authorities arrived. I then drove to Pembroke and phoned Sheriff Sloan and Dr. Renaud.

"Sheriff, I found this empty cartridge on the stairs when I stepped down to the living room." He handed the cartridge over to Sloan.

After the good Father's statement, the three authorities gathered for some coffee in the kitchen.

"Tom, could you ask Father Harrington to have someone fetch us some sandwiches from Chapeau," Mike asked. Hunger was setting in on the men. Tom went outside to speak to Father Harrington.

"So, Mike," said Dom, "Cantin says he arrived after the priest and the priest says he arrived to find Cantin here already. I do not know if that makes a difference, but I have noted it. Cantin does not seem like the brightest guy around."

"Dom," said Mike, "remember on the way in I saw holes in the screen as if bullets had been shot through it? Well, I checked the wall the woman in the living room was facing when she was shot, and I found three lead bullets in it.

"I pulled them out with my jackknife. Looks like .32-caliber rifle bullets to me. I also dug out a fragment of lead from the dining room floor."

Mike then turned the bullet fragments over to Dom, who put them into an evidence box he always carried with him.

After the sandwiches arrived and they had eaten quickly, Dom resumed his interviewing and the constables continued looking around the farmyard.

Third up was Joseph Allard, age 52, farmer and Joseph Bradley's nearby neighbour

Statement from Joseph Allard taken Friday, July 21, 1933, beginning at 1:10 p.m.

In a very stoic manner, he began. "I rose from bed at around 5 this morning. I heard two shots being fired about 6:15 to 6:30 a.m. in the vicinity of Joseph Bradley's house. I did nothing upon hearing the shots." He said he then saw a woman running towards the Bradley house with a man chasing her toward the door. He then heard three or four more shots. He did not actually see the man and woman enter the house. He stopped and looked on, hearing the shots and a minute or two later saw the door and window of the house being closed from inside. As he was finishing breakfast, he saw a man going to the Bradley barn from the house.

The man had a coat thrown over his head and stooped as he walked. The coat was of a yellow shade. The man then walked from the barn to an outbuilding, which was used as a garage. He could not see him again. The man was of medium height and walked bent over all the time.

Fourth up was Adam Allard, bother to Joseph, age 49, farmer and neighbor of Joseph Bradley.

Statement from Adam Allard, taken Friday, July 21, 1993, beginning at 1:50 p.m.

With the same composure as his older brother, he began. "I live 650 feet from Joe Bradley's place. I heard shots and seen the man going to the barn with something over his head on the morning of July 21, 1933. I was there when Father Harrington showed up, but I did not go into the house then."

Fifth up was Narcisse Vaillancourt, age 71, farmer and nearest neighbor of Joseph Bradley.

Statement from Narcisse Vaillancourt taken July 21, 1933, beginning at 2:15 p.m.

After providing his age and name, the frail and timid man began speaking in a very nervous manner.

"I live 250 feet from Joseph Bradley's place and heard rifle shots this morning when he was at his barn. I then saw a woman running to the Bradley house, followed by a man, and heard more shots.

"I became afraid and ran into my own place.

"I peered out of my window and saw a man in the Bradley farmyard. Then I cautiously went around the Bradley outbuildings to Michael (Mick) Bradley's place and met Michael's wife and asked her where Mick was.

"She told me he was in the house, changing his clothes.

"I told her about the gunshots, and she went and told Mick about them.

"Then Mick came out and asked if it was not his Uncle Jack who had done the shooting.

"I told him I do not think so but that it might have been Tom, Mick's brother, who is known to be a bit queer.

"Mick then suggested getting a gang of men together and going to his father's farm.

"Then Mick invited me in for breakfast, but I told him I was too nervous to eat.

"Me and Mick started to walk to Demers Center and someone stopped to give us a lift. Mick, dressed in grey trousers and a blue shirt, intended on going into Pembroke. I then left him and walked back to my place where I met the other fellows."

The sheriff stopped his interviews at this point, unsure if there were other witnesses from the crowd of onlookers wandering idly around the farmyard. He had interviewed the five men who had greeted them when they arrived. It was now near 3:00 p.m.

Suddenly, Constable Tom Belanger burst through the door, with an excited expression on his face. He shouted, "Mr. Cantin has found another body.

"Dom, in the henhouse buried under some hay with blood splatters on the ground, is another man, dead."

Dom and Tom left the house, locked it after themselves, and went to the log henhouse. They entered to see a body with flies and moths circling it. The clucking chickens were running amok. The crowd of men outside the house had followed them to the henhouse.

Dom shouted at Cantin to come in with him and Tom.

"So Cantin, who is this guy?" he asked.

"It's John Bradley, brother to Joseph," said Joseph Cantin.

"Okay, Tom, let's cover this body with whatever you can find," said the sheriff. Tom found some burlap bags and covered the body. They headed back to the house, but not before Sheriff Sloan addressed the crowd of men, grown to about twenty.

"Has anyone seen Michael Bradley around the farmhouse today?" he asked.

No one had.

"I do not want to learn that anyone has gone into the henhouse or the stables. You can stay around the yard, but that is it," shouted Sloan.

"Now I am finished taking statements for today, but if one of you has something to tell me, come see me first thing in the morning."

Everyone nodded their heads that they understood.

When they had returned to the house, Mike was sitting on the porch smoking his pipe. The other two men joined him. Dom filled him in on the new discovery. It was now about 3:30 p.m.

"Dom," said Mike, "while I was looking about, I found a footprint in the ground behind the henhouse. I followed other tracks that lead to Demers Center Road. I followed them along the road bank going south for about 1,000 feet until they ended at some bush. Then, there were broken twigs in the bushes, as if someone had run through them. You know, it was in the direction of Michael Bradley's place."

"Mike," said Dom, "please go back to the footprint and cover it with what you are able to find so that we can preserve it for the detectives.

"Mike, you know Michael Bradley has not been seen all day, even though one of the witnesses told me that Bradley knew very early this morning about the gunshots. Mr. Vaillancourt had gone over to his place around 7 a.m. to tell him. Upon hearing the news, Bradley proceeded to have breakfast and then joined Vaillancourt on a walk to the confectionary at Demers Center without checking after his parents. It seems like the oddest reaction for someone whose family may have been threatened.

"My druthers are that we wait for the detectives before we do anything with Michael Bradley. Approaching him or anyone else there before they are here may screw things up."

"Agreed," Mike replied. At that point, he and Tom turned over the shell casings, one of them still loaded, that the men around the farmyard had picked up.

6

THE CORONER ARRIVES

Dr. Renaud exited his car and joined Dom and Tom on the porch. He was a silver-haired man in his early 50s with a long, smartly trimmed beard. He was always dapperly dressed and was wearing a light tan seersucker suit. The men were all from Campbell's Bay and were on friendly terms.

He apologized for coming late but spoke of other pressing medical duties in Campbell's Bay. He was a doctor first, with lots of patients, and a coroner second.

Mike returned from the henhouse. Sloan filled him in on who the murdered individuals were and where the bodies lay. He told the doctor that the bodies were to remain where they were until the Quebec Police arrived.

Dr. Renaud examined the five bodies, declaring from his initial assessment that all died of bullet wounds. The bodies were beginning to have a smell of decomposing flesh. From the time of their deaths to when a funeral home car came to fetch them, they remained at the farm for 34 hours.

The doctor stated that he would prepare the Bradley home for a Dr. Roussel, medico-legal expert of the Quebec Attorney General's Department, to perform autopsies tomorrow. Dr. Renaud would preside over the inquest to take place some-time in the next couple of days.

At this point Mr. W. R. MacDonald, Member of the Legislative Assembly for Quebec, arrived at the house. He spoke briefly to the four men. He did a walkabout inside the house and around the outbuildings and drove off at 4:30 p.m.

7

THE DETECTIVES ARRIVE

At 5 p.m., a black 1933 five-window Ford pulled into the yard. The car had the Quebec Provincial Police (QPP) markings on the sides. It stopped at the front of the house. Two detectives got out, wearing suits similar to the Campbell's Bay men. Cordially, everyone introduced themselves.

Head Investigator, Sergeant Rene Lassier, was about 5'10" in height, with a beefy physique and a jovial, clean-shaven round face. He would stand out in a crowd because of how strong he appeared. He was about 50 years of age and was from Montreal.

The other detective, Sergeant Detective J. P. Dalpe, had a long face and a well-groomed mustache that covered his thin upper lip. He was about 5'8" tall, with a willowy physique and a very neat appearance. He would stand out in a crowd for how well-groomed he looked. He was from Hull and was also in his 50s.

Lassier had a strong French accent. Dalpe did not. The Sergeant Detective said they would work in the English language as that seemed to be what most people on the Island spoke on a regular basis.

Dalpe was the most renowned detective in the Gatineau and Pontiac areas. In 1929, he had investigated the poisoning of a man by his wife and her boyfriend, resulting in their convictions and subsequent hangings. He also led the investigation into the murder of a lumberjack whose body was found on the Aylmer Road outside Hull in 1932. He had solved many bank robberies and other major crimes.

The detectives were shown the two bodies in the outbuildings. They then went inside the house and looked at the three bodies there. They all sat down at the kitchen table, more coffee was made, and the new arrivals were brought up to date. They were told about Michael Bradley's very suspicious behavior that day.

Chief Investigator Detective Lassier spoke, "Sheriff Sloan, High Constable St. Germain, and Constable Belanger, what you have accomplished so far in this investigation is remarkable. I commend you for establishing the road blocks, taking the very important statements from witnesses, and the findings of the shells and the foot print. The type of massacre that took place this morning is something that we, as experienced investigators, see very rarely in our careers. What I do know is that this will become a spectacle in the next few days as reporters and curiosity seekers from near and far will pour into this area. Please avoid speaking to others, especially reporters. Now we need to give some information, but as a team, we will decide each day what we say.

"We also need to secure the crime scene so that people are not able to just come and go. Mr. St. Germain, please arrange for the Chapeau Constable to post guards around the clock at this farm yard. No one is to be allowed on the property, except for investigators, unless I approve it.

"Clearly, we know who we are going to focus on as the main suspect, and that is Michael Bradley. His suspicious behavior today, particularly in showing no interest as to what happened at his father's place and the tracks that lead to his house, leads me to think he is our murderer. This is the most important thing we keep to ourselves.

"After we have a bite to eat, Sergeant Detective Dalpe and I are going to pay a visit to Michael Bradley and interview whoever is there. I would like you, Sheriff Sloan, and you, Mr. St. Germain, to join us and poke around looking for evidence as we do our interviews.

"We will work until sunset, about 9 p.m., these July evenings. That makes a long day for all of us. We are tired from our drive, and you must be tired from your work today.

"We will not show any hostility toward Michael Bradley. We want his cooperation. Our questions this evening will be asked in a most non-accusatory manner as possible.

"Tom, please stay here and watch over the crime scene. Tomorrow morning, we will check out the footprint and the tracks.

"Thank you for your outstanding diligence today."

Detective Dalpe spoke for a moment. "I also congratulate you for your work today. It is making our jobs so much easier. I think when you're poking around tonight, look for a .32-caliber rifle. These shell casings indicate that is the murder weapon we need to find. Any questions?"

There were none. The men were becoming tired and hungry, so they just found a spot to sit and rest. The Montreal detectives were also fatigued after their long ride, so they found resting spots. All of them were smoking cigarettes or a pipe. Smoke filled the room, masking some pungent smell of dead bodies out of the air.

Sheriff Sloan directed Tom to take his car into Chapeau to book rooms for the detectives and Dr. Renaud at the Grey Hotel and pick up more sandwiches for a quick bite at supper.

"Also, Tom, please ask Andre to remove the road blocks at the bridge. I think we know who we should be focusing on at this point," said the sheriff. "Wouldn't you agree, Sergeants?" asked Sheriff Sloan. Without hesitation, they both nodded in agreement.

Dr. Renaud told everyone that Dr. Roussel was coming to Chapeau that evening and had a room already booked at the hotel.

The sheriff and high constable would return to their homes in Campbell's Bay.

8

MICHAEL BRADLEY

It was 6:30 p.m. when the four authorities met Michael Bradley, a slightly built man, only about 5'8" and 135 pounds, with light brown hair and a heart-shaped, clean-shaven face. He still had on the grey trousers and blue shirt from the morning. He was out in his farmyard and showed no visible alarm when the detectives told him who they were. Introductions were made.

In a very soft voice, he addressed them, "Suppose you are here about what's going on at my dad's place?"

Lassier, showing a friendly demeanor, replied, "So, Mr. Bradley, what do you know so far about what happened?"

"Well, one of my neighbors came over this morning and told me about the gunshots he heard coming from my dad's place. I was too scared to go over there in case the shooter was also gunning for me. I heard this afternoon about the killings from someone else," he replied in a very odd and impassive way.

"Could we talk inside? Mosquitoes will be out very soon as the sun sets," Dalpe asked politely.

"Why, sure," replied Bradley. The five men went inside the small farmhouse and into the kitchen. Inside, they met Bradley's wife and noticed a young teen girl sitting at the top of the stairs.

Curiously, Dalpe asked, "Who is the young girl on the stairs?"

"That is our niece Muriel, who is staying with us to help my wife with our children. Right now, she's getting them ready for bed," replied Bradley.

"So, Mr. Bradley," said Dalpe. "I wish to ask you a few questions, and if you do not mind, Sergeant Lassier will talk with your wife. Sheriff Sloan and Mr. St. Germain are going to look around the house and the yard. Do you have any problems with that?"

Peering around at the four intruders, Mick Bradley hesitated before saying, "No."

While this discussion was taking place, Sloan and St. Germain stepped outside and started towards the unpainted wooden outbuildings in the farmyard to search for clues.

The following is the statement Mr. Michael Bradley, age 43, provided to Sergeant Dalpe of the Quebec Provincial Police during the evening of July 21, 1933, at around 7:00 p.m. He spoke confidently and in an unemotional manner.

"About 7:15 a.m., Narcisse Vaillancourt comes over to my place. I met him in the yard. He had walked across the field to my place.

"I was doing chores. He told me what was going on at my folk's place. I then come into the house to eat my breakfast that the wife had already prepared for me. I invited Narcisse in to join me, but he did not wish to. He was all scared-like. He did, however, have a coffee while he filled me in on more that was going on. After breakfast, I walked with him to Demers Center.

Dalpe asked, "Where did you sleep last night?"

Bradley, trying to figure out what his best answer should be, said, "I slept last night with my wife."

Dalpe asked, "Why were you going to go to Pembroke today?"

Bradley replied, "I was going to go to Pembroke today because I needed to get some medicine for my stomach. I had not worked for my dad since Wednesday."

Dalpe asked, "Are you partner with your dad?"

Michael Bradley

"Yes, I own part of that farm," said Bradley. "I put in $1,800 when it was purchased. My brother Tom, who has some head problems, did not put any money into the place. He does help out with some work. We bought the farm 14 years ago and my father planned to buy more land if we have a good crop this year."

Dalpe asked, "What do you think of the tragedy?"

An emotionless Bradley responded. "You know, I first thought that Tom had gone wild. He acted funny most of the time."

He continued his statement, in a matter-of-fact tone. "I know of no threats to me or my family."

Dalpe asked, "Mr. Bradley, do you own any firearms?"

"I own a .32 special rifle, 1884 model in good shape, and a .32 revolver," Bradley responded. I missed the rifle about ten days ago. I went out hunting when I saw a deer nearby. When I got back, I left the gun on the table. When I got up the next morning, the rifle was gone from the room. The door had not been locked. I'll fetch the revolver if you want it."

Dalpe asked, "Did you have a quarrel with your dad?"

Bradley responded, "You know, my father and I had a few words last fall before we moved. My father thought my children made too much noise in the house; that is why he wanted us to move. At that time, I asked him for a split and to settle up. My father did not say if he would or would not."

The interview concluded about 8:30 p.m. Bradley turned his revolver over to the detectives.

"Mr. Bradley, I'd like a few words with your niece Muriel," said Dalpe.

"Nay, she a young one, and she don't know nothing," said Bradley.

"Mr. Bradley, if you have nothing to hide or worry about, I am sure no harm will come if I talk to her. So, what do you say?" asked Dalpe.

"Aye, it should be fine," said Bradley.

The following is the statement of Mrs. Michael Bradley, age 29, provided to Sergeant Lassier of the Quebec Provincial Police during the evening of July 21, 1933. She spoke slowly and nervously. She was a pretty woman, slight like her husband. An air of gloom hovered over her.

"I got up this morning at 6:15 a.m. My husband got up around 6:30 a.m. We do not always sleep together, especially with this heat and humidity. Last night he slept by himself downstairs.

"Around 7:30 p.m., I saw my husband talking to Narcisse Vaillancourt. Mick, my husband, was out doing chores. That is when I first heard of the trouble. It's so sad. Who would do this?

"I thought it might be my brother-in-law Tom, who was quite queer. My father-in-law should have placed him in a mental institution a long time ago, but they wanted to care for him. My in-laws were decent people," she paused and started to weep.

She gathered her thoughts and continued, "We moved into this place last November when Joseph Bradley asked us to leave because he wanted us to live by ourselves. We rented this place from Mr. Demers, for whom the Center and the road are named.

"My husband and Joseph quarreled about us having to leave. My husband does not talk about money and business with me, so I do not know any more than what I told you already."

Mrs. Bradley continued, "We had a gun around the house that my husband hunted with. It was in the house until about 3 or 4 days ago. He always hunted in the evening after all the chores were done and he'd done his work at his father's place."

She then informed Detective Lassier that in fact her husband had gone over to his parent's place that day to see what was going on. "He went over for only a few minutes and then returned and remained here all day. He had intended to go into Pembroke to buy some Russian Oil because he has a bad stomach and he uses that to help. But with the trouble, he changed his mind."

She finished up at 8:00 p.m. by stating that she washed one of her husband's overalls that day, which were hanging on a chair in the dining room. Detective Lassier then left the house for a moment. He called for Mr. St. Germain and asked him to check out the overalls hanging in the dining room. He then returned to the house.

The following is the statement of Miss Muriel Marchildon, age 14, provided to Sergeant Dalpe of the Quebec Provincial Police during the evening of July 21, 1933, at around 8:40 p.m. She was a pretty, petite girl and very timid when speaking.

"I have been living here for about three weeks. I got up this morning about 6 a.m., the same time as Mrs. Bradley. Mr. Bradley sleeps downstairs sometimes. He slept downstairs last night. I saw him still sleeping when I came downstairs. I could not swear he was sleeping because I just saw the blankets; I just thought he was.

"I know Uncle Mike owns a gun, but he never told me it went missing. When I first saw Uncle Mike, he had his Sunday clothes on. That was when Mr. Vaillancourt came to the house."

Muriel Marchildon

Sheriff Sloan and High Constable St. Germain had returned to the house earlier. St. Germain had examined the hanging overalls and found a .32-caliber rifle shell in the pocket. The overalls were damp. He turned the overalls and the shell over to the sheriff.

The sheriff and the high constable found a large cardboard box with underwear and another pair of overalls with some empty .32 revolver shells in the pockets. They had not found anything in the yard.

The authorities retired from Michael Bradley's home and returned to join Tom Belanger at the crime scene.

They were all tired, so they decided they would meet at 8 a.m. the next day to review everything.

Lassier went to his car and grabbed a mask for Belanger to use overnight to buffer the corpses' smell.

Tom asked the sheriff if they would bring his car tomorrow morning so he could return to Campbell's Bay during the day. The sheriff said he would.

The brief interview ended. Sergeant Dalpe concluded that he had found the weakest link in the family, Muriel.

9

HOME

Dom dropped Mike off at the porch steps at around 10:30 p.m. Mike, my grandpa, wearily climbed up to the porch and walked its length to enter the kitchen where Edna, my grandmother (age 31), was seated at the table. She rose to greet him and asked if he was hungry.

"Edna, if you have some pie, I would love a piece along with a cup of coffee," he said.

She cut a slice of apple pie, placed a scoop of ice cream on top, and poured some coffee from the kettle. She served grandpa at the table and then sat down across from him. She said, "Michael, you look very tired."

"I am Edna," he said. "It has been an extraordinary day with horrific findings and an event that most people think happens everywhere else but never in their own backyard. "I cannot tell you a lot, we have to be careful, though I know you are a woman of great discretion.

"Five bodies were found shot to death at one farm on Allumette Island. Men were standing around gawking. Some went into the house and saw the carnage before we arrived." Mike went on to tell her about the detectives and Dr. Renaud and how Tom stayed there to watch over things.

Sympathetically, Edna looked at her husband and then told him what she learned today in Campbell's Bay.

"I went to mass this morning at 9 a.m. to pray for whatever you were becoming involved in. Father Flanagan told the congregation that something dreadful happened on Allumette Island. He mentioned that some people were murdered.

"Outside, people were asking me if I had heard anything and if you were up there. I told the folks that you had gone up there with Dom Sloan but I really didn't know anything. This afternoon, I went shopping on Main Street. People stopped to ask me the same thing. People are curious and excited. News like this can sure stir things up."

"Edna," Mike said, "I have to walk to Tom's place at around 6:30 a.m. to pick up Tom's car and drive it up to Demers Center. I am not sure if I will be back tomorrow night, but I'll phone and let you know."

On that note, they retired for the evening.

10

MEETING IN THE MORNING
SATURDAY, JULY 22, 1933

First thing that Saturday morning, my grandpa, High Constable St. Germain, phoned Constable Andre Dagenais and told him to organize the Chapeau volunteers so that someone was always watching over the crime scene. He directed Andre to join them at the farmyard where the slaughter took place at the 8:00 a.m. meeting time. He then picked up Tom's car and drove to Demers Center.

All the men were on time, including Dr. Renaud, the coroner. Head Investigator Sergeant Lassier introduced Dr. Roussel. St. Germain introduced Andre, who had brought a volunteer watchman with him.

Lassier told everyone he was needed back in Montreal that day and that he would be departing shortly via the train to Ottawa and then on to Montreal. Sergeant Detective Dalpe would assume command.

After Lassier left, Dalpe spoke to the group. "Constable Belanger, thank you for keeping watch last night. I have brought you some hard-boiled eggs and toast from the hotel to bide you until you get home to your wife's home cooking. You can leave when you want, but please return later today. We need all the help we can get.

"Today, Dr. Roussel will do the autopsies in the farmhouse, so we will all need to assist in bringing the bodies of Mr. Joseph and Mr. John Bradley in from the outbuildings and that of Mr. Tom Bradley from upstairs in the house.

"Secondly, the sheriff and the high constable will join me in detaining Mr. Michael Bradley to officially identify the victims for the autopsy and then as a material witness. It is my plan to hold him overnight at the hotel, so he attends the inquest this evening. He is to be guarded by a constable, and then I will transport him to the Campbell's Bay jail until the inquest is over.

"St. Germain, will you ensure that, when Michael Bradley finishes the identifications, he is taken into custody and a constable is assigned."

The high constable nodded his assent and spoke. "Constable Dagenais, please arrest Mr. Bradley after the identifications and escort him to the Grey Hotel. Hold him until this evening. I will relieve you when the inquest is over."

11

FETCHING MICHAEL BRADLEY

"How are you doing, Mr. Bradley?" Dalpe asked Michael Bradley, who answered the door to his knock at 10:00 a.m. St. Germain and Sloan stood behind him.

Bradley had on a pair of overalls that morning. He replied in a dour way, seemingly more morose than he had been the previous evening, "What can I do for you, Sergeant?"

"Mr. Bradley, we need you to join us and go to your father's farmhouse. By law, an autopsy needs those closest to the deceased to identify them.

"As well, I forgot to ask your niece something last night. You know, so much is going on, a person gets a little forgetful sometimes," Dalpe replied in an offhand manner, as if whatever he needed was not that important.

"I'd think my niece, who is only a child, does not have much really to tell you," said Bradley.

"Now Mr. Bradley," chided Dalpe, "this is an investigation of great importance, and everything we learn from any possible witness needs to be known. So yes, I insist you call your niece now and I will speak to her."

Bradley, his face unreadable, acquiesced and called for Muriel.

Muriel, so slight and timid, came down the stairs. Dalpe asked her to come outside with him to talk. The other men remained back at the doorstep.

In the yard, away from Bradley, Dalpe said in a soft but serious tone, "Muriel, I feel that you did not tell me all that you know last night. There are men and women dead over at the other place, and a very horrible person murdered them— something you know more about then you are letting on. What you know might lead us to him. You're young, and you may believe it's best to keep secrets. But, please pray to your Creator and ask Him if it is not a sin to kill. You know your catechism and you know the commandments, so you know what He will say. So, I ask you, do you want to tell me something?"

She looked at Dalpe with a wan face and started to cry. She ran away from him and into the house.

12

AUTOPSY

Bradley looked stunned at the ghastly sight of the dead bodies. He withdrew a handkerchief from his pocket and wiped his eyes. He murmured, "My, oh my."

He then proceeded to identify the bodies. Once he was done, Constable Andre Dagenais, a handsome young man in his late twenties, approached him and in a commanding voice said, "Mr. Michael Bradley, I am arresting you as a material witness. Tomorrow you will be escorted to Campbell's Bay to be detained at the jail until next Friday. This evening you will attend the inquest into the deaths of your family members, and next Friday, you will be returned from Campbell's Bay for the inquest continuation."

Bradley's face became ashen and his knees buckled slightly. Dagenais then placed him in the car. He allowed Bradley to stop at his home to give farewells and to pick up a few things for himself.

Gathering in the yard was a throng of onlookers and journalists. The onlookers were country folk, the men wearing overalls and the women with short hair wearing plain-colored dresses. The journalists wore suits and carried large boxed cameras. There must have been nearly a 100 people present.

Dalpe approached them, looking to see if he recognized anyone among them. He saw the men from yesterday. He recognized some reporters from Hull and Ottawa.

He approached and addressed the reporters, "Gentlemen, I am glad to see you here. I would like you to inform your colleagues that I will speak outside the Grey Hotel tonight after tonight's inquest.

He then turned his attention to the others. "Now for the rest of you, you must leave this farmyard now. This is a crime scene, and you cannot disturb it. We search it to find clues. So, hear me so that you do not come in conflict with the law. Anyone found on this land, henceforth, will be charged with trespassing and possibly obstruction."

Grumbling, they began to disperse.

Next, Dalpe wanted to see the footprint. He took careful measurements of it, then returned to Michael Bradley's place where he had Mrs. Bradley provide him with a pair of Bradley's boots. He compared his measurements with the boots. He entered his finding in his notebook and took the boots into evidence.

Sloan, St. Germain, and Belanger branched out to canvas neighbors on what they might know.

When they gathered back at the house at 3 p.m., they found Father Harrington there. He was attending to the collection of bodies by the area funeral home. There were a number of hearses in the yard. The bodies had been decomposing now for 34 hours.

Michael St. Germain went to speak with him. "Father, I commend you for looking after this."

Cheerless, the good father replied, "So much tragedy in such a small community. Only God understands the full nature of man and how evil he can be.

"Michael, I have known you a while now. If you remain this evening in Chapeau, I expect to see you at mass tomorrow morning. I say mass at 9 a.m., 10 a.m., and 11:00 a.m. I am preparing my sermon to speak to my people about what has gone on here. I hope it might bring some solace to you and to my congregation."

"Father," said Mike, "I have not missed mass often in my life. This Sunday does not seem like a good time to do so. I'll see you tomorrow."

With that, he joined the others to hear Dr. Roussel's findings

"I will start with John Bradley, aged 65. He has a small wound to the scalp, presumably caused by a blunt instrument. He was shot in the abdomen, which caused his death.

"Mr. Joseph Bradley, aged 69, was shot twice—once in the head and once in the abdomen. The head wound is the cause of death.

"Mrs. Joseph Bradley, aged 69, was shot in the chest. That was the cause of her death.

"Miss Johanna Bradley, aged 37, was shot in her neck and the bullet penetrated her lung. Powder marks around this wound indicate the rifle barrel had been only six inches from the victim when it was fired. That is what caused her death.

"Mr. Tom Bradley, aged 45, was shot twice, one bullet passed through his spine and the second penetrated his back. Either bullet would have caused his death."

Afterward hearing the coroner's report, Dalpe, Sloan, Belanger, and St. Germain huddled for a few minutes.

"Sergeant Dalpe, I think you need to speak to Mrs. Isidore Vaillancourt tomorrow. She wishes to tell you things that she knows about Michael Bradley and his father," said High Constable St. Germain.

With that, the group headed to Chapeau at around 5 p.m. to eat together. During supper, they agreed to drop formalities and began to call each other by their first names. Sergeant Detective Dalpe's name was Jean Paul, but everyone called him JP.

My grandfather called my grandmother to tell her he wouldn't be home that evening. He had decided to relieve Andre, who was watching over Michael Bradley. He would stay with the man overnight.

· · ·

Chapeau had only one phone line. The local operator was backed up with a number of reporters trying to phone their stories in. When my grandfather spoke to the operator, she placed his short call ahead of the others.

13

THE INQUEST

The police officers drove from Chapeau together in Dalpe's car. Nearing Ludger Allard's place, they found cars parked on both sides of the road starting almost half a mile before the farm's driveway entrance and almost a half a mile past the entrance.

There were nearly 300 people gathered in Allard's farmyard. It was a Saturday evening, and this was the best show around. People had come from Pembroke, Fort Coulonge, Waltham, Campbell's Bay, and Chapeau. Reporters were there from as far away as Montreal and Toronto.

The officers stood at Allard's front door awaiting Andre's arrival with Bradley. When his car pulled into the yard, the crowd surrounded it. They were trying to get a peek at Bradley.

Andre parked as near to the house as possible. He got out and went to the passenger side to open the door for the hand-cuffed Bradley and help him out. Flash cameras went off as he stepped out. People leaned toward him to catch a glimpse of his face. St. Germain and Sloan went to Andre's assistance. They tried to keep the crowd away.

Bradley entered the courtroom. He still wore the same over-alls and shirt he had on from the morning. He looked haggard and miserable. He was directed to a seat near where his wife was seated. They embraced each other.

The room was not large enough to fit much more people than the presiding officials, law enforcement, and the witnesses who would be called to testify. There was room for a few reporters. Dr. Renaud had earlier used a straw draw to select the reporters that would be allowed in.

The key witnesses that were seated in the courtroom were Joseph Cantin, Narcisse Vaillancourt, Father Harrington, Joseph Allard, Adam Allard, Mrs. Michael Bradley, Miss Muriel Marchildon, and Mr. Michael Bradley.

Sergeant Detective Dalpe would present on behalf of law enforcement what they had discovered so far.

Dr. Renaud instructed those in attendance on what would take place. He and members of the jury would be posing questions to the witnesses. There was a court reporter in the room to record what was being said. He advised everyone that the next hearing date would be next Friday in Chapeau. He then called Dalpe so that he and the jury could ask questions on the most salient investigated evidence found so far.

Dalpe sat erect on a kitchen chair. To his left was Renaud and the jury and to his front, the others in the makeshift courtroom. He started his presentation.

He recognized the fine work that Sheriff Sloan and the members of the initial investigation had done on the first day. He was emphatic when he declared that the murders were premeditated in the mind of the slayer for some considerable time before the horrific act was carried out.

He reviewed statements from the first day witnesses and gave an overview of some of the clues they had found so far.

He then went to the most prominent findings. He focused on the inconsistencies found in statements taken from Mrs. Michael Bradley, Miss Muriel Marchildon, and Mr. Michael Bradley. He pointed to the differences in Mr. Bradley's story about his hunting rifle going missing 10 days before the murders. Mrs. Bradley had said she saw it just 3 or 4 days before. Miss Marchildon had never heard that it went missing at all. He told Dr. Renaud and the jury that Mr. Bradley claimed he slept with his wife in his bed upstairs the evening before the killings. Both Mrs. Bradley and Miss Marchildon stated that Mr. Bradley had slept downstairs.

Dalpe turned his attention to some clues that had been found. He told them that they discovered shattered shells and broken lead bullets from a .32-caliber rifle, the same type of gun Mr. Bradley says went missing. He informed them that a footprint was left at the scene that measured the same as Mr. Bradley's foot size. He talked about a trail leading away from the henhouse, where one of the bodies was found, toward Michael Bradley's home. Finally, he told them that they had found a .32-caliber rifle shell in a pair of recently washed overalls hanging on a chair in Mr. Michael Bradley's dining room.

The other witnesses followed Dalpe. Their testimony all coincided with earlier statements they made to the law enforcement officers.

Michael Bradley was the final witness. For most of the hearing, Dr. Renaud and the jurors listened attentively and asked few questions. This changed when Bradley sat in the witness chair. Bradley was peppered with questions about the differences in what he said and what his wife and niece had said. Bradley went on the defensive and at one point shouted out, "My wife is mistaken on those things."

Dr. Renaud adjourned the hearing at 10:00 p.m.

14

DALPE SPEAKS TO THE PRESS

It was getting late, but that did not diminish the reporters' enthusiasm as they stood outside the Grey Hotel to listen to Sergeant Detective Dalpe as he provided news that they would report to their readers in tomorrow's morning edition. Most nights in Chapeau during July are hot and muggy. Tonight was no different.

"Gentlemen, thank you for joining me. I know a few of you were at the inquest hearing, so what I have to say will be a bit repetitious for you."

Dalpe repeated much of what he had said during the hearing. He did add the following:

"Mr. Michael Bradley is being held as a material witness. He will be held in the Campbell's Bay jail until next Friday. Our most important need is to find the missing rifle. We will be searching a thick bush behind Michael Bradley's home, the other woods a quarter of a mile away, and the area in the front of his home. While either side of the house is flanked by neighboring farms, there are also a number of thickets, wild strawberry patches, and light underbrushes covering several acres of ground. If necessary, we will tear down outbuildings to find the weapon.

"I will be asking for volunteers to help us look.

"Thank you. I need to get some rest. These have been grueling days for the sheriff, the high constable, and the other fine officers who have assisted us.

"Tomorrow is Sunday, so we will be attending mass in the morning and continue our investigation in the afternoon.

"So, good night."

15

THE STATEMENT

While Dalpe addressed the press, my grandfather had gone to relieve Constable Dagenais. He wished him a good night and then said hello to Bradley.

The room was small, with a single bed and a chair in the corner. There was a small bathroom with a toilet and sink.

Bradley was lying on the bed, reading a recent Ottawa Journal newspaper.

"So, High Constable," uttered a bleak-faced Bradley, "this evening's hearing was not so good for me, eh?"

"Mr. Bradley, there are many clues pointing in your direction. It seems you are not being truthful. There were many contradictions in what you have told and what others are saying," said St. Germain.

Bradley was fidgeting about on the bed. He paused for a minute and then quietly asked if he could give a statement to clarify some details.

St. Germain, adrenalin rising, quickly said sure, but he needed to go down and get Constable Belanger to listen as well.

Belanger joined them, and both men took notes while Bradley spoke. But before he spoke, St. Germain cautioned him, "Any statement you make will be used against you at your trial."

Bradley insisted he wanted to continue. "I went to my father's place around 6 a.m. and met (Joseph) Cantin in the stable. My father came in, and I spoke to him about some money and hay. Then they, my father and Cantin, took pitchforks and chased me out of the stable. I ran into the shed and Cantin jumped up and took a gun and shot John and Joseph."

"Mr. Bradley, we are having difficulty following what you are telling us. Was John also in the stable?" asked St. Germain. Bradley nodded.

"Are you saying you were not in the stable when Cantin shot them?" asked St. Germain.

Bradley again nodded, yes.

"Please continue," St. Germain urged him.

"How the gun came to be in the stable, I do not know," stated Bradley. "That was the first time I seen the gun there. I started to go out of the shed and met my sister.

"She said to Cantin, 'I will get Tom to shoot you.' She ran into the house and Cantin ran after her.

"I hid behind the stable and heard six shots. He came back with the coat over his head and said to me, 'I have shot them all, Mike.' I asked him to let me see the gun, then I told him it was mine.

"He took the coat off and told me to beat it, that he would take the blame. I beat it through the field to my house. I do not know what he did with the gun.

"That is all, High Constable. I did not do it, but I should have told you this at first," finished Bradley.

"So why didn't you?" asked St. Germain.

"I am scared of Cantin and what he might do to me and my family," replied Bradley.

After Bradley's new statement was concluded, St. Germain and Belanger huddled in the hallway outside the bedroom, discussing the new twists in Bradley's story. Incredulously, Mike shook his head, "What a lot of manure!"

Tom replied, "He is desperate, and his efforts to disparage Cantin just show how far he will stoop to escape justice."

"Tom, go get some sleep," said Mike. "We will attend the 9 a.m. mass and then meet up with JP to fill him in. I will sleep in the chair."

16

FATHER'S SERMON
SUNDAY, JULY 23, 1933

9 a.m. Mass at St. Alphonse Parish, Chapeau, Quebec

The law enforcement officers attended the earliest mass. They found seats inside the crowded church. Women, children, and the elderly occupied the church pews. The men stayed outside on the church porch where they smoked pipes and cigarettes and visited with each other.

Father had spent hours preparing his sermon, right into the early morning. He spoke to his flock and to the town's visitors from the pulpit.

"I welcome those people who are visitors to our fair community.

"You are all aware of the horrific tragedy that has come to our small and remote part of western Quebec. Joseph was one of the finest men I knew—trustworthy, honest, and kindly. His brother was so as well. Mrs. and Miss Bradley were very spiritual members of our parish. We all have lost important members of our parish family.

Father Harrington

"God always has his reasons that we fail to understand. It is a mystery why innocent people would be so brutally killed."

He continued on for some 15 minutes, expressing his view that the parish and community would survive this tragedy.

"We must join as one and pray. We must rely on, care, and be kind to one another."

He concluded by informing them that the five people killed would be laid to rest that evening.

17

BREAKFAST

Dalpe, Sloan, St. Germain, Dagenais, and Belanger were all seated in the Grey Hotel dining room eating breakfast and drinking coffee.

The Grey Hotel

Dalpe started the conversation. "Gentlemen, I have some unfortunate news. Sergeant Lassier has been withdrawn from the investigation. His workload in Montreal is too heavy for him to continue here. I am now the head investigator of the case. It is now just our small group that will have to manage this case." Dalpe continued, "Today, I plan to interview Mrs. Narcisse Vaillancourt, as you recommended, Mike."

Mike advised the group that Michael Bradley was sent, accompanied by a constable, to Campbell's Bay to be detained there in a jail cell. He also told them about Bradley's voluntary and very incoherent statement pointing a finger at Cantin.

Dalpe said, "Dom, please do some follow-up with Cantin. I really doubt that he did the killing. Mike, please take some of your men and search Joseph Bradley's property and the bush and fields around there. Dom and I will check out Michael Bradley's place."

They left the dining room and went on their way.

Dalpe drove out to the Vaillancourt farm and knocked at the door. A grey-haired woman, in her late 40s, opened the door.

"Good afternoon, ma'am. I'm Sergeant Detective Dalpe from Hull and head investigator of the brutal murders of your neighbors."

"Well, I am Mrs. Isidore Vaillancourt, and I have been expecting you," she replied.

The following is the statement Mrs. Isidore Vaillancourt, age 49, provided to Sergeant Dalpe of the Quebec Provincial Police during the afternoon of July 23, 1933, at around 1:00 p.m.

"I have been doing chores for Michael Bradley for over a year now. Last year, Mick Bradley told me that he had put money in the farm and done work on it but could not agree with his family and had been told to take the road. He also said every time he went to his father's, his sister insulted him.

"Yesterday, the morning after the murders, I had a talk with Mick Bradley.

"He told me he'd fooled the detectives by telling them his rifle had been stolen 10 days before. I told him he needed a better lie.

"He told me that his sister, Mrs. Crowley, and her husband would want money now that all the rest are dead.

"There are quicker ways to take these people than to use the law.

"I know people are saying the killer wore a long coat over his head. A while back I gave Mrs. Bradley an old army coat. I told her to cut it up and make something for her kids. I'd get that from Mrs. Bradley."

Sloan and Dalpe met at Michael Bradley's place. The sheriff went to the door and spoke to Mrs. Bradley. She told him she did not know where the coat was.

Dalpe spotted Muriel in the yard and gave her a warm smile. The girl just looked away.

St. Germain advised that he had about 30 men search the areas around the farms and found nothing. He told them he was returning to Campbell's Bay for the evening.

On Monday, July 24th, efforts were continued to find clues, but it was not until the following day that the most important evidence was discovered—the rifle.

18

RIFLE
TUESDAY, JULY 25, 1933

St. Germain had his volunteer search party down to 18 men today, retracing their steps from the previous days. They checked the fields and bush around Joseph Bradley's and Michael Bradley's farms.

In the meantime, Dalpe and Sloan spoke to more possible witnesses in the nearby farming community.

In mid-afternoon, Dalpe and Sloan pulled into Michael Bradley's place. Sloan asked Mrs. Bradley if she would mind talking to him. She agreed.

Dalpe approached Muriel and asked her to come and sit in the car. He wished to speak to her. Reluctantly, she got in and sat beside Dalpe who sat in the driver's seat.

He turned and looked kindly at her small face, aware of her considerable apprehension about speaking with him. Softly, he asked her, "Have you thought about what I said to you the other day?"

She murmured, "Yes."

"Muriel, I do not wish to say you were lying, but you are not telling me everything that you know," said Dalpe.

Warily, she nodded and silence set in for a couple of minutes. She finally broke the silence with an agonizing expression on her face. "Sergeant Detective Dalpe, I was told by my uncle and aunt to say what I did," she said.

Dalpe murmured, "Go on."

"Before 7 a.m., I met my uncle crossing a field near his home. He (Michael Bradley) told me that if anyone asks her, he had not been out," recounted Muriel. "My uncle then went toward the cowshed, and later Mr. Vaillancourt entered the yard."

Dalpe asked, "What was he (Michael Bradley) wearing?"

Muriel responded, "He was wearing overalls with a black smock, tan shirt, and rubber gumboots."

Dalpe asked, "Did you see any blood?"

"I did not," Muriel replied. "I then saw him come from the cow shed with a parcel in his hands."

Dalpe asked, "Did he change his clothes before Mr. Vaillancourt met with him in the yard?"

"Yes," said Muriel.

Dalpe asked, "Did you see a rifle around the house before the shooting?"

"Yes, a few days before," she replied.

Dalpe asked, "Where did your uncle sleep the night before the shootings?"

"Downstairs," she replied.

Dalpe said, "Thank you, Muriel." She returned to the house.

Dalpe got out of his car and stood looking at the barn. Sloan joined him.

"Dom, from what Muriel has told me, he went into the cowshed when he came back over that field," said Dalpe. "That was around 7 a.m. and the shooting took place earlier than that, more toward 6 a.m. So, when Muriel saw him crossing the field, it was the second time he was returning from his father's."

Dom interrupted him to add, "I read Mrs. Bradley's statement, and she had mentioned her husband had gone over there briefly that morning, something he failed to tell us. She let it slip and now we know the significance of that."

"Precisely Dom, she knows the truth and has been protecting her husband," said Dalpe.

"I surmise that he had returned to his father's place to hide in the bush to see Father Harrington and the other four neighbors gather at his father's place. He was curious about their reaction to what they would find. And then he saw Mr.

Vaillancourt heading his way, so he hurried back to his yard.

"When he was returning from there, he met Muriel and then went to the cowshed. We have searched everywhere but his outbuildings for the rifle. I bet he hid that rifle in the cowshed. He would've headed there on his first return; I'm certain of that."

Sloan fixed his eyes on the cowshed and blurted out, "Well, I'll be! You are on to something."

They hurried to the cowshed and went inside. Soon St. Germain and Belanger joined them. The cows were in the field, so that made things easier. They hunted for the rifle among the hay, in boxes, and in the cow bales.

Sloan was poking around when he noticed an area in the dirt floor where it appeared some digging had taken place recently. With his hand, he dug down and retrieved a buried box of cartridges. Dalpe then saw another spot with loose earth and he dug down. There it was—the rifle—the proof and the sound of Mr. Michael Bradley's death knell.

The search was called off, and everyone headed out. Dalpe needed to get the rifle and cartridges sent to Montreal to be examined at the crime lab.

"Dom, the cartridge box shows that these were sold in Pembroke," stated Dalpe.

. . .

"OK, Dom, while I arrange for the rifle to be sent, please go to the hardware store in Pembroke and see if the store clerk remembers selling the box of cartridges to Michael Bradley.

"Mike, before I send in the rifle, we will take a photo of it. You can show the photo to Bradley's neighbors and see if they recognize the rifle. It has a special leather strap that should help identify it."

19

MORE EVIDENCE

Sheriff Sloan drove to Pembroke, Ontario, part of his trip by way of the ferry that provided service to travelers in that direction.

He stopped at the Bank of Nova Scotia, where Thomas Bradley had a bank account. He met a William Grayson, a bank clerk, who informed him that Thomas Bradley had $1,192.12 in his account. He said he didn't know if Michael Bradley knew of the account.

He met Mr. Alexander, a Royal Bank clerk, who told him Joseph Bradley had $239.56 and Johanna had $142.96 in their accounts.

He drove to meet with Mr. J. Blakely, a hardware merchant in the town. He showed him a picture of Michael Bradley and asked him if he had sold him the box of .32-caliber rifle cartridges. He could not identify Mr. Bradley but said the box, with his store's labelling on it, would have been sold at his store.

Sheriff Sloan stopped to see Napoleon Lafrance, an insurance agent. He was the agent on record that facilitated the purchase of the farm by Joseph Bradley 14 years earlier. The sale price was $14,000, and he (Lafrance) still held a $4,000 mortgage on it.

Lafrance told Sloan, "In 1918 when old man Bradley bought the farm, farming was expanding from farmers just growing food for themselves to growing surplus to sell for cash and profit. The war had created a big demand for more food. Bradley bought the farm when prices were high. For the next number of years, his farm did well, and he diligently made his loan payments. Once the depression hit, he could not sell surplus like before and he started to fall behind in payments. The old man and his son Michael found some work off the farm with highway maintenance crews. This helped them out a bit.

He told Sloan that Michael Bradley had come to see him a year ago and asked him to divide the farm between him and his father. He advised Bradley he could not legally do that. He also informed Bradley that his father was behind in payments and interest but that his father had told him he was getting $1,000 from Michael to make a payment and catch up. He told him he might foreclose on his father.

Meanwhile, High Constable St. Germain went to farms near Michael Bradley's house and showed pictures of the rifle. Mr. Demers, who had known Michael Bradley for 14 years and who was his current landlord, identified the rifle as that owned by his tenant. He knew the weapon quite well because of the leather band wrapped around the barrel.

His son, Albert Demers, joined them. He said he'd borrowed the rifle from Michael Bradley two weeks ago to do some hunting and had returned it. Albert had also lived for four months at Michael Bradley's place during which time he saw the rifle many times. "It is Michael Bradley's rifle," declared Albert.

20

BRADLEY CONFESSES

That morning Dalpe moved out of the Grey Hotel and drove to Campbell's Bay. He found a room at the Campbell's Bay Hotel for the night.

He then met Constable Belanger and went to the jail to meet Michael Bradley. Bradley was sitting in his cell, looking impassive and disheveled. Bradley had signaled via Belanger that he wished to speak to Dalpe. He wished to confess to the murders.

"Good morning, Mr. Bradley," Dalpe fixed his attention on Bradley. "You wished to speak to me?

"We have found your rifle where you hid it. As well, your niece has told us of your whereabouts the morning that your family was murdered."

Silence ensued. Bradley looked first at Belanger and then at Dalpe. His expression turned to pain and his face became pale. He remained seated.

Dalpe continued, "Mr. Bradley, I am going to ask you to fess up and tell the truth for the first time. Constable Belanger will stay and listen to what you have to say. Anything you say will be repeated at your trial. You do not have to say anything. We can leave now. But, I have been investigating for many years and feel that the evidence is so stacked up against you that we now have a "Fait accompli."

"Sergeant Detective, if I tell you what happened, will things go better for me?" asked Bradley.

"Mr. Bradley, I cannot tell what a Justice will decide," said Dalpe. "That is up to the court. But think of your wife. I am pretty sure she has been protecting you. She has lies on her conscience now. By confessing, you will ease her burden. She does not have to continue to support your ruse."

Bradley looked to the ceiling and contemplated his next move. Finally, he confessed with the following:

"I do not know why I accused Cantin. I was the man who covered my head with the coat.

"I got up early in the morning and went to my father's farm. When I got there, my uncle opened the stable door. I thought it was my father, so I shot him and dragged him into the henhouse and covered the body with hay. Then my father appeared, and I shot him. Then my sister came along, shouting that she was going to get Tom to shoot me. I chased her to the house and shot her through the door of the living room. I then turned around and shot my mother. I went upstairs where I shot Tom.

"I pulled the blinds in the house down and went out, pulling the coat over my head. I proceeded to my own house through the field where I left the coat in a gully.

"I went home where I put the gun and the box of cartridges in holes that I dug in the cowshed dirt floor.

"I returned to my father's place and saw the men that had heard the shots gather in front. I watched them for a while and then ran across the field back to my place.

"I met Muriel as I left the field and entered my yard. I told her that, if a man comes and asks if I have been out, to say no.

"I then had my wife wash my overalls. My wife had nothing to do with this."

Dalpe asked, "Why?"

Bradley replied, "I had helped buy the farm, but my family was pushing me out. My father would not let me use cut wood from his piles. My sister was always mean to me. We had to move, and I needed to pay rent for my house, and then my father asks me to give him $1,000 to pay off late mortgage payments and accumulated interest. My father made all the decisions, some bad ones that cost us, and he wants more money from me. He doesn't listen to me about farming things, and we might lose the farm. I'd had enough."

Dalpe and Belanger left a shaken Bradley in his cell.

For reasons known only to Dalpe and Belanger, no signed written record of the confession was made.

Sloan arranged for the constable to fetch the coat in the gully where Bradley said he had discarded it.

21

SUPPER AT THE ST. GERMAIN HOME

My grandmother met grandpa at the door. She asked him what his day was like. He replied that it had been very fruitful. The case was solved, and now it would be up to the court system to decide Mr. Bradley's fate.

It was about 5 p.m. He told my grandmother he was meeting Sergeant Detective Dalpe for a beer at the Campbell's Bay Hotel Beverage Room.

My grandmother suggested he invite Mr. Dalpe for a homemade supper. She had pork roasting in the oven. There was lots to go around. She would put their best chinaware out for the dinner. Grandpa thought it was a very good idea.

He met Dalpe at the beverage room where they each ordered a quart of Dow Ale. Dalpe was most pleased with the invite and cheerfully accepted.

Smoking and drinking, they lauded their collective's efforts to solve the crime. Dalpe told my grandfather that he'd obtained a confession. He had already told Sloan, who was almost ecstatic about their success.

"He is a good man, your sheriff is," said Dalpe.

"Yes, he is that," replied my grandfather.

They finished up, and then proceeded to the St. Germain home, where Dalpe quickly fell under my grandmother's inquisitive eye.

While she served her guest, the four children, including my mother, were seen but not heard from.

"Sergeant Detective Dalpe, it is not often we have a visitor of your stature to our table," she said.

"Mrs. St. Germain, it is not often that I am fed by such a beautiful and wonderful hostess as you," replied Dalpe.

My grandmother cheerfully replied, "I have heard of the flattery from the men of Hull."

During supper, my grandmother showed no hesitation with her questions about Dalpe's personal life.

Grandma asked, "Are you married?"

"I was but my wife fell to cancer several years back. She was a wonderful wife to me and an incredible mother to our five children. They have all grown now. My girls are married and have provided me with grandchildren. My only boy is a doctor in Montreal. He is the oldest. My wife was proud of her children," stated Dalpe.

"Sergeant, how did you learn to speak such good English?" asked grandma.

"Actually, my mother was Scottish, and my mother tongue is English. I learned French from my father and outside of the home," responded Dalpe.

During supper, my grandmother continued with her questions. Finally, my grandfather butted in with, "Edna, I think our guest might now prefer being questioned in the courtroom or by reporters than to answer any more of your questions. Perhaps you should begin to put the children to bed."

My grandmother blushed and rose from the table.

Dalpe also rose and said, "Mrs. St. Germain, the meal was exquisite and your conversation makes my heart warm for the days I sat around the table with my wife and my children. You have brought me such fond memories this evening, and I thank you for that."

With that she hastened the children upstairs, and my grandfather went to his liquor cabinet and drew out an aged bottle of Scotch.

Sipping on their drinks, they spoke about detective work and crimes that they had investigated in their career. My grandfather was due in court soon to testify about a bigamy case involving an area farmer. Dalpe had been involved with investigating organized crime in the Hull-Ottawa area.

Dalpe became quite somber when he turned the conversation back to their current one.

"Most murders are done by person or persons who are known by their victim or victims rather than strangers. In this case, I believe Michael Bradley felt that his family members were not living up to his version of what a family should be like. His disappointment that his father was not fair in his dealings with him despaired him so much his anger turned to rage and then murder. He also felt hopeless as the threat of a foreclosure hung over the family farm. His father made all the important decisions.

"He will hang, be assured of that. News of the killings has reached most households in Quebec and Ontario, and people will be clamoring for his head. And when the time comes for his hanging, your village, where the hanging will take place, will become a focal point for people to gather and participate in the spectacle."

On that note, Dalpe said his good evening and returned to the hotel.

22

INQUEST PART 2

FRIDAY, JULY 28, 1933

The crowd was now near 700 persons waiting outside the Chapeau Community Center where the inquest was scheduled to start at 3 p.m. They waited in hot and humid weather. Dark and threatening clouds covered the village.

Michael Bradley arrived with a lawyer, a Mr. J. Ernest Garboury of Quyon. He had previously been the county prosecutor. He was only representing Bradley on this day for the inquest.

The crowd was so dense that Bradley had to be brought into the court through a back entrance to avoid any disturbance.

Nearly 400 people were allowed into the hall to watch the proceedings. All the reporters were able to be seated. W. R. MacDonald, MLA, was also present.

Dr. Renaud addressed the public who had been allowed in and packed every inch of the hall. He welcomed the residents of Chapeau and vicinity. He believed they had been aroused by the tragedy and wanted to see justice done. He called the murders the worst crime to ever happen in the Pontiac.

Dr. Renaud then called the proceedings to order. He reviewed the evidence from last Saturday's hearings and then began to call witnesses.

St. Germain, Belanger, and Sloan provided updates on their collection of evidence.

Dr. Roussel presented his autopsy findings.

The reappearance of Miss Muriel Marchildon as a witness set off a buzz of whispers in the room. She told her revised story. She was cross-examined by Mr. Garboury.

Dalpe then took the stand where he spoke about finding the rifle. He told the coroner and jurists that the Montreal crime lab confirmed that it was the rifle used in the killings.

Albert Demers identified the rifle as the one owned by Michael Bradley.

Michael Bradley sat in his seat with a dejected look about him. He looked gaunt, his hair unkempt, and a handkerchief wrapped around his head.

Mr. Garboury asked Bradley if he wanted to address the hearing. Bradley said he did not wish to. Dr. Renaud said that he could not compel Bradley to speak.

The hearing had taken one hour and fifty minutes.

The jury withdrew for deliberations. When they left, the crowd inside rushed to the doors to get outside and away from the heat inside the room. Rain started dripping from the sky, making the air outside cooler. The crowd filled the side street beside the hall, waiting for a decision. Bradley had been taken to a side room in the hall guarded by two husky constables. He just sat there with his head down, a forlorn sight.

After 50 minutes, the jury returned with their verdict.

"We hold Michael Bradley criminally responsible for the deaths of Joseph Bradley, Mary Bradley, John Bradley, Johanna Bradley, and Thomas Bradley at or about 6:30 a.m. on July 21, 1933, at their place of residence at Demers Center from wounds inflicted by a .32-caliber rifle owned by Michael Bradley."

As the charge was being called out, a sudden furious squall of rain burst from the sky, sending the crowd scattering for cover. Thunder rumbled, and lightning lit up the skies. Bradley was taken out the back way, and the constables drove him directly back to Campbell's Bay and the county jail.

23

PRELIMINARY HEARING
SEPTEMBER 7, 1933

Justice Roland Millar presided over Michael Bradley's preliminary hearing at Campbell's Bay in the Pontiac District Court on a charge of murdering his 5 family members.

Bradley, wearing a freshly pressed suit, sat in the courthouse guarded by Constable Tom Belanger. Belanger had paid for the pressing out of his own pocket. Bradley was represented by lawyers James Crankshaw and Marcel Garboury from Montreal.

James Crankshaw of Crankshaw and Crankshaw was a partner with his father. He was one of the foremost lawyers in civil and criminal matters in all of Quebec. He was aged 51 during the time of the Bradley trial. He was a handsome man with an athletic build. He had defended murderers since the age of 25 and had occasionally won acquittals for his clients over the years. He was also a well-known rugby player in Quebec.

While awaiting his hearing, Bradley had spent his time at the Campbell's Bay jail sleeping 12-13 hours a day. He refused the opportunities to take exercise in the jail yard. He was allowed any foods he'd desired, but he opted to avoid meats, tea, or coffee and ate only vegetables and fruit. He was polite and quiet in jail. His wife visited twice during his incarceration. He saw his lawyers and priest regularly.

Sheriff Sloan and High Constable St. Germain were required to assign a special squad of officers to keep order inside and outside the courthouse due to the huge crowd that had gathered there by 8 a.m. When the courtroom door was opened for spectators, the crowd pushed from the outside, causing people to tumble over each other and fight to get in and find a seat. The special officers pushed the crowd back once all the seats set aside for spectators were filled. Sloan went out to inform the crowd that the courtroom was filled and that no one else would be let in.

The Justice finally called Bradley into the courtroom at noon. Somewhat pale, he stood in the prisoner's box where he stayed while all the witnesses seen at the inquest were called to testify. Mr. Marcel Garboury, cousin of the lawyer Mr. Ernest Garboury from Quyon, cross-examined witnesses, particularly Muriel Marchildon. She remained consistent with her last testimony at the second inquest.

After hearing all the witnesses, the defense team argued that the trial be held in Campbell's Bay rather than in Hull, the preferred location of the prosecution team.

Justice Millar formally committed Michael Bradley to a murder trial to be held in Campbell's Bay in the new year.

After the hearing, Bradley was escorted to Bordeaux Jail in Montreal. He would stay there until July 1934, when his murder trial was convened in Campbell's Bay, Quebec.

II

CAMPBELL'S BAY MURDER TRIAL

24

TRIAL EXCITEMENT BEGINS
JULY 12, 1934

My grandmother went to the grocery store. Her sister Jean (my great-aunt) and her husband owned the store. She approached Jean, who was behind the counter. The store was very busy, as visitors to Campbell's Bay were on the rise.

"Jean, can you break away for a few minutes?" asked my grandmother.

Jean arranged for her husband to come out from their residence at the back of the store. The two sisters sat in the kitchen sipping on tea.

"Edna, it is really getting crazy these days with people coming into town in droves. The two hotels are filling up and local folks are taking in short-term boarders. There are signs on front windows inviting people to stay with them."

My grandmother, with trepidation showing on her face, replied, "Michael is worried about bad sorts joining the frenzy and causing village people trouble. Villagers do not lock their doors at night. They should now because their places might be broken into. Shop owners like you need to be on the alert for thievery."

"We are doing just that," said Jean, "but we have noticed that some people are not paying for things they take when the store is open. I hope Dom and Michael place more special constables on the street day and night."

"I'm sure they will, but they have to swear in these special constables and pay for their time," said Edna. "I understand the sheriff's budget is pretty slimmed down these days."

Jean added, "The bright spot in all of this is that we have never done so much business during the depression. I wonder where people get the extra money to travel and stay here."

Edna shook her head, grabbed her purse, and said goodbye to her sister.

Campbell's Bay Courthouse and Jail

25

TRANSPORTING MICHAEL BRADLEY
SUNDAY, JULY 15, 1934

Michael Bradley rose in his cell at 7 a.m. He ate his breakfast and then met his lawyer, Marcel Garboury. Bradley had gained some 28 pounds in jail and looked strong and healthy.

Garboury was in his early 20s and had recently graduated from law school at McGill University. He was a junior in the Crankshaw and Crankshaw law firm. He was short in stature but owned a booming voice. He was a nice-looking fellow with short buzzed hair, an eager face, and sharp eyes, good for trying to look into a person's soul. Some years after the Bradley trial, he would become Commissioner of the Quebec Provincial Police.

"You will be sent in handcuffs to Campbell's Bay and accompanied by two armed guards. Please do not discuss your case with anyone besides Mr. Crankshaw and me. Understood?" asked the young lawyer.

Bradley nodded his head, acknowledging that he understood.

At 8 a.m., two muscled guards came for him and placed him in a police vehicle. They stopped once in Hull for lunch and then arrived mid-afternoon in Campbell's Bay, where Bradley was placed in a jail cell.

His wife came to the jail and met with him for a while. It had been some time since he had been able to see her, because she had no way to get to Montreal.

Mrs. Bradley had to move out of the rented farm property and, with their children, had moved in with a family member.

26

TRIAL'S FIRST DAY
MONDAY, JULY 16, 1934

Campbell's Bay Courthouse

Francois Caron, Prosecutor

Hundreds of people were gathered outside the courthouse as early as 7 a.m. on the first day of Michael Bradley's murder trial. They stayed there until the doors were opened at 9 a.m. Those lucky to get in would have to wait until 3:30 p.m. before the first witness testified. Jury selection needed to take place first. It was another hot, muggy July day in Campbell's Bay, and many of the people inside used hand-held fans to try to keep cool. Men wore their best suits, and women wore their best summer dresses in the hot courtroom.

Mrs. Bradley did not go inside. She sat in a chair in the courthouse lobby. People she knew, and people she did not know, stopped to wish her well.

Justice Philemon Cousineau was presiding over the trial. Francois Caron, Crown Attorney for the Pontiac, was prosecuting the case. Marcel Garboury and James Crankshaw, defense councilors, represented Bradley.

Francois Caron had been Crown Attorney for Pontiac County since 1929 and resided in Campbell's Bay. He knew Sloan and St. Germain quite well. He had a handsome face and was of average height and build. He was known as being fair-minded and having a brilliant legal mind. He was not a showman in the courtroom.

Justice Cousineau's first ruling was that only officials such as Sergeant Detective Dalpe, Dr. Roussel, and Dr. Renaud would be allowed to be in the courthouse during deliberations. Other prosecution and defense witnesses could attend only when they were called to testify.

James Crankshaw challenged the fact that Sheriff Sloan was involved in the jury pool. The Justice had two newspapermen empowered to determine if the selection of the jury pool had been fair. They brought in a ruling that they could not believe that partiality entered into the selection of the pool.

Mr. Garboury asked the Justice to rule that defense witnesses would receive the same treatment as the prosecution's in terms of being reimbursed for expenses. The Justice ruled they would be treated the same.

The jury comprised W. I. Bolen, Quyon; George S. Lucas, Bristol; Irvin Brownlee, Shawville; John Clark, South Onslow; Charles Meyer, Bristol; Moise Chevrier, Quyon; Richard Armitage, North Onslow; Everett Steele, North Onslow; Frank McKinnon, Campbell's Bay; Edward Brownlee, Clarendon; Alexander McDonald, Quyon; and Napoleon Chabot, Bristol.

These men came out of a pool of 44 possible jurors. They had been chosen after Mr. Crankshaw asked each whether they had any preconceived opinion as to the guilt or innocence of his client.

After the selection of the jurors, Mr. Garboury went out to the lobby to confer with Mrs. Bradley. He wished to know if any of these men had a grudge against her husband. She knew of none.

Mr. Caron, prosecutor, addressed the jurors at the outset. He explained the principal factors of the murder case to be submitted to them by the Crown. He told them that it was the most important case ever tried in the Pontiac County.

First, he told them that the Crown must prove that certain persons were murdered. The Crown would then produce drawn plans of the site where the murders occurred, portions of shattered rifle bullets in the home of the accused, and eyewitnesses to certain occurrences at Joseph Bradley's homestead on July 21,1933.

Mr. Crankshaw's opening remarks pointed to the law as it relates to reasonable doubt.

Joseph Cantin, the excitable WWI veteran who had worked for Joseph Bradley at the time of the murders, was the first to testify at 3:30 p.m. Witnesses continued testifying until 6 p.m.

During the day, Michael Bradley was under perfect self-control and followed the evidence with but passive interest. He smiled at times over situations that arose during the day.

27

SECOND DAY
TUESDAY, JULY 17, 1934

Mrs. Bradley entered the courtroom on the second day and sat at the back. The courtroom was filled again. There were more ladies attending on this day than the first.

Six witnesses testified that day, including my grandfather. He pointed to the bullet fragments and empty shells he found at Joseph Bradley's place. He testified to the effect that he found a pair of overalls in the cowshed containing several .32-caliber cartridges for a revolver. He found a second pair hanging in the dining room, which were damp and had an empty .32-caliber cartridge in one of the pockets. This cartridge would fit the rifle.

The trial adjourned at 5 p.m. until 10 a.m. the next day.

James Crankshaw, Defense Attorney

Marcel Garboury, Defense Attorney

28

THIRD DAY
WEDNESDAY, JULY 18, 1934

Sergeant Detective Dalpe took the stand on this day. While being questioned by Prosecutor Caron, Mr. Crankshaw began to interrupt and object to what Dalpe was saying whenever he tried to speak to the three statements Michael Bradley had given during the investigation, the initial interview, the false accusation against Joseph Cantin, and the confession.

The lawyers then met with the Justice in his chambers to argue the admissibility of the statements.

Justice Cousineau ruled that they were inadmissible except Mr. Bradley's interview before the inquest. He told the courtroom:

"After the evidence before me on this point, I think there is no doubt that on July 21st and 22nd, the accused was under the guard not strictly under arrest but under the keeping of either St. Germain or Dalpe. I think that all declarations after the beginning of the inquest before the coroner should be rejected because the warnings should have been given by the coroner himself."

The rest of the day was spent on testimony as to the finding of the rifle and the financial status of the deceased parties.

Mrs. Bradley spent most of her time sitting in the lobby but was seen on occasion standing at the rear of the courtroom.

Michael Bradley's demeanor indicated he seemed to be taking in the proceedings with merely a casual interest.

29

FOURTH DAY
THURSDAY, JULY 19, 1934

Michael Bradley entered the courtroom, unshaven and sleepy looking.

Despite the continuing blazing heat and humidity, the crowds outside and inside remained large. The crowd on this day included the Pontiac County Member of Parliament, Charles Belec.

The witnesses from the earlier hearing continued to be called. This was the day the prosecution's star witness was testifying.

Muriel Marchildon, seemingly as big as a minute, sat in the witness box and began her story for the people inside the courtroom.

She told the courtroom that she had been living at her aunt and uncle's as a maid for three weeks before the murders happened.

She said Uncle Michael sometimes slept upstairs and sometimes on the ground floor. He had been sleeping on the ground floor almost every night of the week that the murders occurred.

Muriel said she had gotten up about 6 a.m. on the day of the murders. She did not know when the accused got up. She first saw her uncle about 7 a.m. that day, walking toward the stable. She related that he told her to tell the person who was coming to the house (Vaillancourt) that he had not been out at all.

She told the courtroom that Michael Bradley was wearing a brown shirt, overalls, and gum-rubbers. He had taken off his overalls and shirt and placed them beside the stove. They had been wet. She could not recall if he had done this before in the three weeks that she had been with them. Mr. Caron raised the three articles for Muriel to confirm they were what he had been wearing.

She said that she had seen the .32-caliber rifle three days before the shooting.

To Mr. Caron she explained her different versions of the events at the first inquest hearing and admitted to her meeting with Detective Dalpe between the two inquest hearings. She had told different stories because her aunt had told her not to say anything about the gun.

The day ended at 5 p.m.

Father Harrington had testified before Muriel. When he exited the courthouse, he was approached by a number of reporters attempting to coax a word from him. He responded by chastising the curiosity seekers who had come to Campbell's Bay for the trial.

"I am appalled that human beings would be so entertained by the misfortunes of others. I ask these people to please show a little dignity and respect toward the deceased from the Bradley family and to Michael Bradley's wife and children.

"The church is open for them to come in and pray for their souls and for justice to be had on earth and in heaven.

"That is all that I have to say."

30

FIFTH DAY
FRIDAY, JULY 20, 1934

Overnight the rain had come and brought cooler weather to the village. Crowds continued to gather in the morning in hopes of sitting inside the courtroom.

Testimony had gone from evidence from those who were at the scene and clues the law enforcement officers had found after the murders to witnesses that described the strained relationship between Michael Bradley and his family.

Bradley sat in the prisoner's dock listening to witnesses describe violent altercations between him and his father. One such occasion was when they came to blows in the cowshed. Neighbors told the courtroom about loud arguments full of cursing by the accused and his family members.

This latter testimony brought the courtroom spectators forward in their seats to lean against the brass rail in front of them.

The accused looked worried on this day. He remained unshaven and tired-looking.

When the Crown rested the case, it had called 28 witnesses in total and provided a lot of hard clues as evidence.

Bradley left the courtroom at the conclusion of the day looking dragged and worn out.

31

SIXTH DAY - TRIAL CLOSINGS
SATURDAY, JULY 21, 1934

Exactly One Year after the Murders

Mr. Crankshaw made a motion to the Justice on the grounds that the Crown failed to prove its case and that there was not one bit of evidence that the crime was committed by the accused. The Justice dismissed the motion. At this point, the defense announced they would not call any witnesses.

The Crown prosecutor commenced his address to the jury at 11:45 a.m.

"I feel that the hand of God left marks by which the author of these could be traced.

"The accused had an interest in his father's farm and had lived there for two years.

"A year earlier, the accused started telling neighbors of the disagreements at home. He asked Napoleon Lafrance, who held the mortgage on the home, to divide the farm between himself and his father.

"He was forced to leave his father's home because of constant bickering. Neighbors heard violent quarrels where Michael Bradley could be heard swearing.

"He had put his money and labor into the farm just to be turned out. He had told a neighbor, a year earlier that he was thinking of killing himself.

"He told Mrs. Isidore Vaillancourt that there were quicker ways than the law to settle matters. People have often taken justice into their own hands for less provocation than this.

"Two shots were fired in the barn and two bodies were found there; a man was seen chasing a girl to the house, and a few minutes later, more shots were heard.

"The murderer had run and walked in a stooped fashion and covered his head with a coat to avoid being identified.

"The bodies in the barn had been moved and covered with hay, showing the murderer had taken precautions.

"I will say that this murder was not an accident. It was too big a massacre. There were two killed and then three to cover up the act. At the house, the windows and doors were closed, just as a precaution.

"Further, the man went to the barn with something over his head to see if everything was covered there for the time being.

"Here I will say that the Crown has produced no eye witnesses. When something is done with care, there is nothing but circumstantial evidence. It is not necessary to bring any direct evidence.

"The rifle was found at the home of the accused, and the shells and bullets were matched to this rifle. I submit that these points constitute a strong case against the accused.

"Evidence shows that the murder was premeditated and done with care.

"Michael Bradley got up in the morning, and no one knew where he went. He saw a man walking toward his yard that morning and told Muriel Marchildon not to say that he'd been out that morning. Instead of greeting the visitor, the accused went into his house and changed his wet clothes.

"He told his visitor, Mr. Vaillancourt, that his brother Tom probably did the killings.

"The coat was found that was used to cover his head. He owned the coat.

"The shoe print found at the murder site measured in size with Michael Bradley's gumboots worn by the accused that morning.

"Two key witnesses, Mrs. Isidore Vaillancourt and Miss Muriel Marchildon, have been cross-examined by the defense and were unshakeable in their testimony. Do you wonder why Miss Marchildon's story was different the first time she testified. Imagine how frightened she must have been, living under the same roof as a man who murdered five people.

"You are sitting on one of the most important cases in Canada, and you have the responsibility to rule as the evidence has proven, guilty.

"Thank you for your attention throughout this lengthy trial."

Mr. Crankshaw commenced his address at 2:30 p.m.

"The killing of the Bradley family was an atrocious crime, and if its perpetrator was brought to justice, he should be convicted.

"Having said that, I do not believe that the Crown has proven my client was that perpetrator. Proof of guilt must be made to convict an accused of any crime with either direct or indirect proof. The latter is called circumstantial evidence, and the chain of evidence is no stronger than its weakest link.

"Surmises and theories are not the proper kind of proof on which to base a verdict. All facts placed before the jury must be compatible with one hypothesis and one only, that of guilt. In the present case, the facts admit a hypothesis of innocence, therefore, there is no case to be sent before the jury.

"Though I believe in the innocence of Joseph Cantin, the Crown and its investigators could have found a damaging case against him, but they did not pursue the investigation in that direction. I am just saying this hypothetically.

"These crimes were the act of a madman. The only motive of the murders on the part of Michael Bradley was a disagreement between the accused and his father. That is not a motive for a slaying."

While Mr. Crankshaw was speaking, a large black bird flew in through the open window behind the jury and struck the wall on the far side of the room close to where Michael Bradley was sitting in the prisoner's box. It caused quite a commotion in the courtroom until it flew out another open window.

Unfazed, Mr. Crankshaw continued, "Mr. Thomas Bradley's financial records show no motive to kill him. The same was for his father, who still owed money on the farm.

"There exists a chain of suspicion, but not a chain of circum-stantial evidence.

"As for Mrs. Isidore Vaillancourt and the statements she said were made to her by my client, I say to you to be careful of the frail memory of a woman with a vivid imagination.

"As for Miss Muriel Marchildon, she has changed her story but only after subsequent meetings with Detective Dalpe who, I believe, suggested the new story for the young woman.

"In my experience, there are more lies told under oath than on the street.

"I'll concede that the shells found by the police were fired by that rifle, but we have no proof Michael Bradley pulled the trigger.

"I suggest that the rifle was planted in the accused's cowshed by someone other than the accused.

"As for the footprint, I wonder how one could have existed after a heavy rain that day, which would have wiped out all traces of a print. It was supposed to have been seen on sandy soil.

"I too wish to thank you jurors for your attention to the trial details.

"You are to render an honest and frank opinion in your verdict. The prisoner at the bar is declared innocent until declared guilty, and he is entitled to the benefit of doubt. I have utmost confidence in you that you will find him innocent."

Justice Cousineau provided the charge to the jury with relevant law as it pertains to murder.

"It is now my duty, after the able addresses of counsels, to give you direction as to the law which applies in this case. I will not refrain from congratulating the attorneys for their pleas.

"In certain cases, murder may be reduced to manslaughter. Discussions, family quarrels, which may have occurred in the family, cannot reduce the crime of murder to manslaughter. There are only two verdicts, guilty or not guilty.

"If there is any reasonable doubt that the case has not been proven, the benefit must be given the accused. Did the Crown prove its case against the accused?

"A case may result in three things, direct evidence, circumstantial evidence, and declarations, confessions or omissions. I think it may be said that there has not been direct evidence of killing. Nobody has seen or recognized the party who has done the killing. The question of direct evidence must be put aside.

"As to circumstantial evidence and declarations admitted to the case, I will touch on those briefly. As to circumstantial evidence, there is no doubt it must be accepted by the jury with utmost care. Circumstantial evidence must be like a chain which binds the accused at the time of the crime. If there are any weak spots in circumstances, that evidence cannot go as far as conviction of guilt. Circumstantial evidence may be corroborated by other elements of proof— declarations by the accused which were introduced in evidence.

"The day after the shooting Michael Bradley went to the home of Isidore Vaillancourt, and what did he tell her? He told her, she said, that his rifle had been stolen about 10 days earlier to which she told him he better tell a better lie than that.

"About Joseph Cantin, we had his evidence. It has been admitted he was going to get some work at the Bradley home. He was told by someone that two shots had been heard and he afterwards heard three more. He went with others and discovered the bodies. The gun was found later in the barn of Michael Bradley. A box of bullets was also found. The question that you must ask yourself is, who controlled possession of the gun at the time of the shootings? It is in evidence that Muriel Marchildon had been working at the home of the accused and had seen the gun and recognized it in court. The gun had been hung in the house of Michael Bradley. That does not prove that Michael Bradley had the gun on the morning of the shooting.

"You are to decide whether the gun was in the possession of the accused at the time of the killing.

"Remember, there are only two verdicts, guilty or not guilty."

Justice Cousineau's charge was completed by 5:07 p.m. He adjourned the trial to 8 p.m. to allow the jurors plenty of time to reach a verdict.

32

THE VERDICT

At 8:15 p.m., the jury filed in just after Michael Bradley appeared, guarded by two men. A minute later, Justice Cousineau took his place on the bench.

The clerk, Alphonse Martineau, asked the jury if they had found the prisoner guilty or not guilty. Foreman John Clark stood up before a packed crowd sitting so still you could hear a pin drop.

"We have not reached a decision as yet."

The courtroom spectators moved about in their seats and loud whispering could be heard throughout until the Justice silenced them with an order.

The defense wanted an adjournment until 11:00 a.m., Sunday, but the prosecution wished the jury to return to immediate deliberations.

Foreman Clark asked if a certain question could be put to the Justice and the lawyers. Justice Cousineau said, "No, I think I have provided you with adequate instruction."

Mr. Clark asked the Justice to repeat the law in regard to verdicts and the Justice replied, "I don't think I have the right to repeat what I have said once."

Mr. Clark then asked for more time and the Justice gave them until 10 p.m.

At 9:55 p.m., the jury returned to the courtroom where Michael Bradley sat awaiting his fate. While waiting during jury deliberation, Bradley was seen playing cards with his guards in the holding room. Mr. Clark rose before the Justice and replied to the question about reaching a verdict with a negative.

"I do not believe this jury can reach a verdict" declared Foreman Clark.

"I do not see any reason for giving you any more time after that declaration. Jury is discharged," ruled Justice Cousineau.

The Justice then ordered Michael Bradley back to the Campbell's Bay jail and returned to Montreal tomorrow, where he would be held at the Bordeaux jail until a retrial was scheduled.

Mr. Caron will lay the question of a retrial to the Quebec Attorney General Department, and the disposition of the case will be decided upon sometime in the near future.

Michael Bradley left the courtroom seemingly relieved but showing little emotion.

33

BEVERAGE ROOM TALK

Dalpe, Caron, Sloan, St. Germain, and Belanger entered the packed men-only Campbell's Bay Hotel beverage room. Some men got up from their table to give it to the lawmen out of respect for them.

A couple of reporters in the room came over to address them. They told them that they had heard rumors that there had been one juror who had been adamant that the Crown had not proven the case beyond a reasonable doubt. It had been, based on rumor, an 11 to 1 vote for guilty.

The lawmen ordered beers, and each drank their first one quickly and then ordered another round. They were quiet at first.

Caron started the conversation, "I am truly disappointed that this happened after placing before the judge and jury such a solid case. The turning point was when the Justice ruled against hearing Bradley's confession. That would have made it a slam dunk."

Tom asked Caron, "Will the same Justice preside over the retrial? Seemed to me, his charge favored Bradley."

"You know the Justice just addressed the law as it pertained to the case; he never commented about the soundness of testimony or clues, so it was an impartial address, from my perspective. Though not permitting the confession in was wrong. In answer to your question about who will preside over a new trial, the answer is, no. A new Justice will be appointed.

"I am going to ask for the retrial to take place in another location. I believe that the juror or jurors who could not convict were influenced by the accused being one of their fellow county men. It does not take much for a juror to be convinced, in his own mind, that an injustice is taking place and it's his duty to prevent it," Caron concluded.

Sloan, Belanger, and St. Germain finished their second beers, said their good nights, and headed home, leaving Caron and Dalpe at the bar.

III

RETRIAL

34

MONDAY, JANUARY 6, 1935

The retrial was taking place in Hull, Quebec, at the Court of King's Bench and presided over by Justice Louis Cousineau (not to be confused with the first Justice Philemon Cousineau). The change in venue had been granted early by a Quebec Justice.

Hull sits across the Ottawa River from Ottawa. It is predominantly a French-speaking community. Its population in 1935 was around 20,000 people. Hull's bars were legally allowed to remain open until 3 a.m. It was primarily known for its nightlife. There were many dim-lit taverns in old buildings and nightclubs that had attracted entertainers like Louis Armstrong. Hull was once one of the most crime-ridden cities in Quebec.

Jury selection was made, and the proceedings commenced.

Michael Bradley sat in the prisoner's dock dressed in a neat blue suit, clean shaven, and appearing healthy. He had paid close attention during jury selection.

His wife was in the courtroom on the first day. She occupied a front-row seat in the spectators' section. She glanced at people in the courtroom she knew and gave them friendly nods. She was dressed in a dark coat and red hat. When her husband had entered the courtroom, she looked directly at him and they exchanged a smile.

In January, it is cold in Hull, so there were no outside crowds like those that had formed in Campbell's Bay during the summer trial. However, the courtroom was overflowing with spectators. So great was the crowd that the huge beams holding up the floor of the courtroom bent slightly under the weight and cracked the plaster on the ceiling of the floor below. However, the beams of the old courthouse were sound and withstood the strain.

The jury was composed of Foreman Ernest Overton, John Shouldice, Philoxime Fournier, Williams Brooks, Henry J. Cross, Walter Bourgeau, Ken McClelland, F. C. Roy, Aime LaFrance, Gerald A Poole, James Arbuckle, and Russell Ormond. They were all from Hull and district.

The Crown was again represented by Mr. Caron. Ernest Bertrand from Montreal joined him on the prosecution team.

Mr. Caron outlined his witnesses and the evidence he would be presenting. His address to the jury was very short.

Hull Courthouse 1895

35

CONFESSION ADMISSIBLE
TUESDAY, JANUARY 7, 1935

Sergeant Dalpe took the stand, and immediately Marcel Garboury objected to Dalpe testifying about any conversation he'd had with Michael Bradley. Garboury argued that the reporting of any conversations with the accused was illegal and asked that the Justice not permit it.

Caron and Garboury then started a prolonged argument about it. Justice Cousineau finally stopped them and told them he would rule on it in the afternoon. Dalpe continued his testimony on other items, like the finding of the rifle, etc.

After a lunch break, the jury was asked to retire while the defense counsel questioned Dalpe about his interview of Bradley in the Campbell's Bay jail. Garboury, who was taking more of a lead counsel role than at the Campbell's Bay trial, asked why an official signed statement from the accused was not taken as it had been at the Grey's Hotel by High Constable St. Germain.

Dalpe replied that he was called to meet Mr. Bradley at his request. When Bradley started talking about having committed the murders, Dalpe only had his notebook with him for taking notes about what was being said.

He warned Bradley that, what he was saying, would be used in court. He made neither promises nor threats to the accused. He asked Bradley if he had any suspicions and other questions. Dalpe told the defense and Justice that Bradley insisted on confessing.

When asked by Garboury why he detained the accused right away before the inquest, Dalpe answered that Mr. Bradley's statements about his whereabouts and the missing rifle and his general disinterest in the wellbeing of his family after hearing that something had happened to them had raised red flags so that he felt it prudent to hold Mr. Bradley in detention.

Justice Cousineau ruled that the statements were admissible. He ruled all statements or confessions by the accused were made voluntarily. Upon hearing the ruling, Bradley was found unable to sit still in the prisoner's dock. He appeared nervous and his hair was tossed and hanging downward.

36

BRADLEY STATEMENTS AND CONFESSION

WEDNESDAY, JANUARY 8,1935

The jury heard St. Germain, Belanger, and Dalpe report that the accused initially tried to point the finger of guilt at Joseph Cantin and subsequently confessed to the five murders.

The other previous witnesses testified as the trial moved quicker than the first.

Hull Quebec Rue Principle 1920

37

THURSDAY, JANUARY 9, 1935

The Crown rested, and the defense called witnesses this time. They did so in an attempt to have the jury bring forward a verdict of not guilty for reason of insanity or a verdict of guilty of manslaughter.

Six witnesses testified of instances where Michael Bradley had been ill-treated at the hands of his father and sister.

Mrs. Isidore Vaillancourt, who had testified for the Crown, now testified for the accused. She told the court that Michael Bradley had suffered from stomach problems two weeks before the killings. Bradley had told her that the doctor had recommended brandy and eggs, but that fresh ones were the best. Fresh eggs were hard to come by, but his sister had plenty. His sister Johanna had refused to give him any.

Joseph Allard, nearest neighbor to the Bradley farm, testified that the accused was not allowed to eat with his family when he was over there working and had to bring a meager lunch of bread and butter and eat in the shed or in the barn.

Allard said that Michael was the only one who really worked on the farm, and he worked far too hard, considering his stomach ailments. His father also refused to repay him what he had invested in the farm or divide it.

Allard had heard Joseph Bradley tell his son that he had never done a good day of work on the farm.

Joseph Cantin told of a tussle he saw between father and son.

And so it went for the remaining defense witnesses.

The defense then rested its case.

38

CLOSING ARGUMENTS

Crown Closes

Ernest Bertrand, Chief Crown Attorney for Montreal who helped Mr. Caron with the trial, quoted from legal works that irresistible impulse was not insanity according to Canadian Law and cited pronouncements of several Justices to that effect.

"Any man is supposed to be sane unless the contrary is clearly proved."

Mr. Caron then commenced his address to the jury.

"It is not necessary for me to go through the whole case when it has been admitted that Michael Bradley did kill those people.

"When the defense said for you to bring a verdict of not guilty by way of insanity or guilty of manslaughter, they do not deny that he did the shooting.

"It was necessary for the defense to bring witnesses to state that Bradley was not in his right senses at the time of the crime. However, Father Harrington said Michael Bradley was not a quarrelsome type but rather a sober and quiet man.

"You have all the evidence that the accused took many precautions so as not to be discovered. The little mistakes he made do not show that he was insane, but that he acted just like any other sane man in the commission of a crime.

"It has been proven that Michael Bradley was on his father's farm for 14 years. It has been proven he put money toward the farm. He was putting everything into the farm, so that when he would be having a conversation about his troubles, it was always included, i.e., when his father, being quite tempered, put him out. It is against the law and society for anyone to take the law into his own hands, but 8 weeks before the crime, he said to Mrs. Vaillancourt, 'There is a quicker way than the law to deal with them.'

"He is not an insane man. He had a reason. He wanted the property, and he premeditated the crime. The only reason he killed his mother and brother in the house was to destroy evidence of the shooting of his sister in the dining room of the home. Everything Bradley did proves he is sane.

"The crime was cold-blooded murder, not after provocation, but done with premeditation.

"Thank you for your diligence and attention during the trial."

Defense Closes

Mr. Garboury had taken the lead at the retrial and was there to provide the defense closing arguments.

In his booming voice, Mr. Garboury said, in opening, that this was his first murder trial.

Quite forcefully, he continued, "There is no clemency for the crime for which my client has been charged should you, the jury, return a guilty verdict. You may bring a verdict of insanity or manslaughter."

Garboury then cited the Criminal Code defining manslaughter, emphasizing the element of provocation.

"If you come to the conclusion that he is insane and you return a verdict accordingly, the court will deal with him so there need be no doubt in your mind whether or not to return such a verdict.

"Could the man who committed this crime be in his right mind? No sane man would pick that time of day in broad daylight to do a thing like that.

"If he were not insane, he would pick the dead of night for the commission of the crime. Something must have happened to Bradley that morning to do such a thing.

"Do you think a man in normal senses would bring the gun right back to his own place when he could have hidden it in the muddy gully between his home and that of his father's, where it might never have been found? There is another thing. He hung up his clothes to dry in the kitchen of his home in full view of everyone.

"Was there provocation? From what you heard this morning from defense witnesses, there was provocation. Michael Bradley's life was an unbroken sequence of sad events. He did all the work. It was he who gave all his money to the family. It was he who slaved and never made a gain.

"He was provoked to run around on a shooting rampage that he did not realize he was doing.

"I ask you that, if you have any doubt, please give my client the benefit of that doubt.

"Thank you."

39

A VERY DIFFERENT JUSTICE'S CHARGE

Speaking eloquently, Justice Cousineau commenced with, "I thank the counsels for their very kindly reference in their conduct of this case."

He then read the formal charge that accused Michael Bradley of committing the five murders.

"Three verdicts would be admissible in this case, the first being guilty as charged, guilty of manslaughter, and if the charge of murder is not satisfactorily proven, a not guilty verdict.

"The punishment for murder is death and, in the case of manslaughter, a penalty of life imprisonment.

"For manslaughter to be considered, there must be sudden provocation, and the act must have been committed before there was time for his passions to cool.

Justice Louis Cousineau

"It is easy to explain this case in a few words, because there is no doubt about the man killing these five people. It is Michael Bradley.

"We have had his confession to the deed placed before us in evidence. The testimony given by Dr. J. M. Roussel and the photographs of the rifle breech-block and the shell cases corresponding prove that Michael Bradley's rifle killed the victims. Scientifically, no other gun could have accounted for their deaths.

"The defense frankly recognized that the killing was done by the man he is defending. The defense submits that the man was so provoked that he lost control of himself. You will have to examine these circumstances. It is true that Michael Bradley didn't receive from his father and sister the treatment that he as entitled to receive from them.

"This man has certainly suffered, not only physically but mentally and morally, at a time when he was in ill health. He must have dreamt of the wrongs that he had suffered.

"At other times he might not have been able to sleep on account of turning over in his head the injustices to which he had been subjected. This may explain why he slept downstairs.

"Possibly after a sleepless night, he got up and went to kill his father, the man whom he believed responsible for his suffering. In the stables, the wounds of the two victims who died there and the marks of bullets on the woodwork explain the situation as to how the shots were fired. He waited, knowing his father would come to the barn.

"His uncle entered the barn first, and it is possible that he shot his uncle by mistake for his father. Even granting the mistake, it was murder providing, of course, that Michael Bradley was sane.

"The father came into the barn next, according to what we know from the evidence. There was a shot. It looks as though the father turned his head to see where the shot had come from and then received a second bullet through the head. This was the second murder.

"His sister Johanna appeared to have been coming towards the barn, and there is strong reason to believe that he tried to pull her into the barn. If he had succeeded in this, the third murder might very well have been the last one.

"Now I ask you, would an insane man wait until Johanna got out into the opening and into the house before he killed her. If he were acting in a fit of passion, would he not have killed her outside the building? And now we come to Mrs. Joseph Bradley. In all his life of ill treatment, have you heard the slightest reference to any grievance existing between Michael Bradley and his mother? Has there been any evidence that she had interfered with Michael? Not the slightest bit of it.

"Admitting that he had been provoked by others and boiling mad at the time, can you (raising his voice) 'Can you give me any explanation of a man killing his mother without even giving her a chance to cry for mercy?' Her toothbrush was in one hand and a glass of water in the other when the body was found, as we have heard in evidence.

"If the accused had been insane, would he have remembered there was still another person upstairs, his brother Tom. He went upstairs and killed Tom Bradley against whom he had no griev- ances, and then he carefully closed the doors and the windows so that people from outside would have less chance of knowing what had been going on. Could you come to the conclusion that these precautions would have been taken by a crazy man?"

Justice Cousineau then defined insanity as laid down in the Criminal Code and remarked that perhaps the best test of whether a man is insane, when he commits a certain act, is whether all recollection of that act is wiped from his mind.

Michael Bradley had been standing, listening to all this with a pale face. Suddenly he collapsed and slumped to the seat in the prisoner's dock.

Justice Cousineau paused and looked at Mr. Garboury. He announced that there would be a 10-minute break so that Mr. Garboury could bring his client to better health. Water and some biscuits were fetched for the accused, and he regained his senses.

Resuming after the 10 minutes, the Justice continued, "We must consider the length of time between the provocation and the criminal act, and analyze the state of mind of the accused. Provocation must be sufficient to deprive a reasonable man (not necessarily the accused at the bar) of his self-control before a murder charge can be reduced to manslaughter. The longer the time, the less reason to consider provocation. In such cases, where much time had lapsed, it is revenge not provocation.

"Remember, you have sworn to return a verdict in accordance to the evidence. No feeling of sympathy may inspire that verdict. Remember those who were killed, those who had the full right to live.

"Your verdict must be unanimous, and the accused has the benefit of doubt.

"Thank you."

40

THE VERDICT

It took the jury 30 minutes to reach a verdict. Michael Bradley, who had been pale and shaken throughout the day, waited nervously in the prisoner's dock when the jury reentered at 5:57 p.m. He slumped back in his seat, shifted nervously, and repeatedly ran his hand through his thick hair. He collapsed once more and slid in a dead faint on the hardwood seat. The doctor declared it was a natural reaction to the strain of the trial.

The Justice again provided a 10-minute adjournment while a doctor checked on Mr. Bradley. Water was provided, and Bradley came to his senses.

The courtroom with nearly 300 hundred spectators, including Mrs. Bradley who sat in the front row, became silent.

Mr. H. J. Kearney, Court Clerk, asked, "Are you agreed on your verdict? Is the prisoner guilty or not guilty of the crime for which he is indicted?"

The Foreman spoke these words, "Guilty of murder."

The courtroom's silence was broken and a loud murmur rose upon hearing the verdict. Mrs. Bradley was seen silently crying in her seat in the front row.

Mr. Garboury, already standing, shouted out, "I ask for a poll of the jury."

Each juror responded, "Guilty of murder."

Bradley fainted again. This time there was no rush to check on him. He lay slumped on the floor of the prisoner's dock. When Garboury noticed him, he rushed over.

The Justice spoke these words to the jury, "You have rendered great service to society, and I believe your verdict is the only one you could have made in accordance with the evidence. Sentence will be pronounced in five minutes.

41

SENTENCING

There was only one sentence befitting this crime, death. For the five minutes that the Justice was in his chambers, he dressed in the clothing appropriate for a death sentence. He wore a black cornered hat and black gloves, denoting the pronouncement of a death sentence.

The Justice shouted for silence to the exuberant crowd. He then spoke to the accused who was semiconscious and slumped in the dock seat, being held by the arms by two guards, "Have you anything to say as to why a sentence of death should not be pronounced on you? If so, now is your opportunity to offer it."

Garboury leaped to his feet in a last-ditch effort to save his client.

"Your Lordship," he protested, "do you expect a man in that condition to make any answer to that question?"

"No," responded Mr. Justice Cousineau, glancing at the inert form of the prisoner. "It is not necessary."

In a deep, firm voice he spoke. "You shall be taken to the prison in the district of Pontiac at Campbell's Bay whence you came, and on the 5th day of April within the walls of that prison in which you shall be confined, you will be hanged by the neck until you are dead. May God have mercy on your soul."

Many doubted Bradley heard these words. The blood had drained from his face, and his eyes were only half open.

A sudden break from the Justice's ordered silence happened when the crowd erupted into a loud restlessness, with people climbing on chairs to view the fainting prisoner and others who had surged against the brass courtroom rail dividing the lawyers' section from the spectators. There were cries of sympathy for the accused and for his wife. Commands from the Justice for order went unheeded.

Finally, the doctor who had helped earlier came to Bradley's assistance. He took the tie from Bradley's neck and opened his shirt. A cold cloth was placed over his face and his color began to return. Father Harrington, who had remained throughout the trial, came over to hold Bradley's hand and provide some encouraging words. Father Harrington then went to Mrs. Bradley's assistance. She was still uneasy and crying.

Bradley was taken from the courtroom by his two guards. When he was back in the holding room, coffee and sandwiches were given to him. He was soon speaking to his guards in a friendly manner and seemed to have recovered from his ordeal.

42

SPEAKING TO JOURNALISTS

Mr. Garboury was surrounded by reporters when he came out of the courtroom. It was a blustery and cold January day. He had his coat on and was holding his hat on his head with his hand so it would not blow away in the brisk wind. He spoke briefly.

"I will continue the fight to save Mr. Bradley from the gallows. It was a pitiful case, and I intend to take all the ways and means to save him. Beyond that, I have nothing else to say."

Mr. Caron then spoke to the crowd.

"I believe justice for the five dead people has been rendered. He did the murders from a premeditated state of mind, and now he must pay the price for it. I believe that, even without his confession, the evidence was there to convict him. But his confession was the most important information the jury heard.

"The Attorney General's Office will make arrangements for the sentence to be carried out. Sheriff Sloan and the jail authorities in Campbell's Bay will be busy arranging for the April 5, 1935, day. Thank you."

43

MEETING THE ATTORNEY GENERAL

My grandfather, along with Sheriff Sloan and Constable Belanger, were invited to eat at the Ritz Carleton Hotel in Montreal with the Premier and the Attorney General of Quebec, Louis Alexandre Tashereau. Francois Caron and J. P. Dalpe joined them. They drove from Hull to Montreal after resting overnight.

The Ritz Carleton Hotel was built in 1912. During the depression many rich people sold their bigger homes and took up residence in the hotel. Many well-known people could be seen in the lobby and in the restaurants.

Mr. Tashereau thanked the men for their dedicated service, recognizing that it took two-and-a-half years to obtain justice. He spoke of how important it was to prove the Quebec Justice System could withstand the international attention that this macabre event brought to it. Bringing closure to it would be welcomed by Quebec citizens.

And so went the evening of fine dining followed by cigars and sherry. The men of Campbell's Bay returned to their homes the following day.

Ritz Carleton

44

FINAL CHAPTER – THE HANGING

Michael Bradley was not immediately returned to the Campbell's Bay jail as ordered by the Justice. He was held in the Montreal Bordeaux Jail until 12 days before the hanging.

On March 24, 1935, he was transported from Montreal to Campbell's Bay and turned over to the authorities there. Twelve policemen accompanied him from Montreal to Campbell's Bay.

Sometime in the mid-1960s, it was my grandmother who told me about the uproar the hanging caused during the week prior to Friday, April 5, 1935.

Reporters came from everywhere, including the USA and overseas. Residents of the Pontiac treated Friday like a statutory holiday. People skipped work to come into the village. Bars were full of revelers.

Village restaurants and shops overflowed with customers. Main Street was full of fancy cars from the cities like Montreal, Ottawa, and Hull.

That week, Mrs. Bradley visited her husband often. So did Father Harrington. My grandfather stopped by to share a few words with Michael Bradley.

During the lead-up to the hanging, a petition had circulated through the Pontiac asking for the Attorney General to commute the death penalty to life in prison. The petition had been signed by many Pontiac citizens. The Attorney General did not respond to it.

April 5, 1935

Bradley's execution was conducted under the supervision of Chief Deputy J. Belanger of Montreal and Sheriff Dominique Sloan of the Pontiac County. Mr. Ellis was the executioner.

Other officials present were Prothonotary A. Martineau; Governor A Moileau of the Campbell's Bay jail; Coroner Renaud; Joseph Mousseau, Governor of the Hull Jail; Father Harrington, curator of Chapeau and spiritual advisor to Michael Bradley; Sergeant Detective Dalpe; and High Constable Michael St. Germain.

A coroner's jury was there as well. Serving on it was F. E. Henderson; A. Ranger; P. J. Mousseau; Percy Smith; Fred Martin; Leo Lemarre; Donat Leguerriere; and P. Shea.

Michael Bradley walked to the gallows on his own accord. The trap door was sprung at 5:57 a.m., and he was pronounced dead at 6:04 a.m. by Dr. Jerome Kelly.

My grandmother told me she heard the trap door open from their house. She said she had never forgotten that thudding sound.

SOME AFTER NOTES

This book's research focused on the reporting from the Ottawa Journal, the Ottawa Citizen, and the Montreal Gazette. The reporters wrote colorful and complete daily articles during the investigation, the inquests, the trials, and the hanging. The daily newspapers sold for 2 cents each in 1935.

There are no reports of what happened to Mrs. Bradley and their children after her husband's death.

Mr. LaFrance, who held an outstanding $4,000 mortgage on the farm, foreclosed in 1934 and sold the farm for $212.00. In 1918, it had cost $14,000. One of the workhorses was a prize stallion that was sold for breeding purposes for $274.00.

My grandfather served many years as high constable for the County of Pontiac. He died at age 79 in 1965.

Sheriff Dominque served as sheriff of the Pontiac County for 26 years. He died in 1961 and was succeeded by his son, Joe.

Father Denis Harrington served as curator of Chapeau until 1940. He joined the Canadian Armed Forces as a chaplain with the rank of Major. He returned after the war to Chapeau as curator until he retired in 1971; he passed away in 1987 at 90 years of age.

Both Justice Cousineau's continued serving the Hull and Pontiac areas for many years after. It is unknown if they were related.

Mr. Caron rose to senior positions in the Quebec Attorney General's Office, remaining as a prosecutor until he retired.

Mr. James Crankshaw passed away in his early 60's and is remembered as one of the great lawyers in Quebec history.

Mr. Garboury served as Commissioner of the Quebec Provincial Police Force for a few years.

When my grandmother passed away, my mother found greeting cards from Sergeant Detective Dalpe to my grandfather from 1935 and on. They had maintained their friendship over the years.

The farm land is still called the Bradley farm, even though a Bradley has not owned and lived there for 87 years.

ABOUT THE AUTHOR

The very successful Allumette Island Massacre and Three Other Canadian Crime Stories was Keith Landry's first full length book. He decided to remove that book from publication and do a moderate rewrite of the Allumette Island Massacre story and publish the story on its own. Readers provided feedback that it was that story that drew them to the book.

Keith was born in Aylmer, Quebec and raised in Ottawa. He met his wife Vivian in Regina where they now live. Vivian is a critical partner in the book proofing and editing.

Other books Keith has written:

Dalpe's Crime Chronicles
Murder Tales from the Archives
The Boarding School at the end of the Dirt Road
Motley Crooks
Dalpe and the Nazi

Keithhlandy.com
All books are available at Amazon.ca